Idaho

Travel Guide 2024-2025

A comprehensive Handbook includes information on the best places to stay, when to visit, activities to do, and things to explore when visiting for the first time.

By

James Jeffrey

COPYRIGHT PAGE

CHAPTER ONE..**5**

1. Introduction to Idaho... 5

1.1. Geography and Climate... 6

1.2. History and Culture... 8

CHAPTER TWO..11

2. Planning Your Trip.. 11

2.1. When to Visit.. 11

2.2. Transportation Options... 13

CHAPTER THREE.. 15

3. Top Destinations.. 15

3.1. Boise.. 18

3.2. Sun Valley.. 19

3.3. Coeur d'Alene.. 20

CHAPTER FOUR.. 23

4. Outdoor Activities... 23

4.1. Hiking and Camping... 24

4.2. Skiing and Snowboarding.. 26

CHAPTER FIVE..**28**

5. Wildlife and Nature... 28

5.1. National Parks and Wildlife Refuges.. 30

CHAPTER SIX...**33**

6. Idaho's Culinary Scene... 33

6.1. Local Cuisine and Food Festivals.. 34

CHAPTER SEVEN...**37**

7. Events and Festivals... 37

7.1. Idaho Potato Harvest Festival.. 38

CHAPTER EIGHT..**40**

8. Accommodation Options... 40

8.1. Hotels and Resorts.. 42

CHAPTER NINE..**44**

9. Practical Information... 44

9.1. Visa and Entry Requirements.. 45

9.2. Health and Safety Tips.. 46

CHAPTER TEN...**49**

10. Idaho for Families... 49

10.1. Family-Friendly Activities... 49

CHAPTER ELEVEN...**51**

11. Idaho for Adventure Seekers.. 51

11.1. Extreme Sports and Thrilling Activities.. 53

CHAPTER TWELVE..**56**

   12. Idaho for History BuffsBoise.. 56

   12.1. Historical Sites and Museums... 58

CHAPTER THIRTEEN...**60**

   13. Idaho for Nature Enthusiasts... 60

   13.1. Birdwatching and Wildlife Viewing.. 62

CHAPTER FOURTEEN..**65**

   14. Idaho for Foodies...65

   14.1. Farm-to-Table Dining Experiences.. 66

CHAPTER FIFTEEN..**68**

   15. Idaho for Solo Travelers...68

   15.1. Solo-Friendly Destinations and Activities.......................................70

CHAPTER SIXTEEN...**73**

   16. Idaho for Budget Travelers.. 73

   16.1. Affordable Accommodation and Dining Options.............................. 75

CHAPTER SEVENTEEN..**78**

   17. Idaho for Luxury Travelers... 78

   17.1. Exclusive Resorts and High-End Experiences................................. 80

CHAPTER EIGHTEEN...**83**

   18. Idaho for RV Enthusiasts... 83

   18.1. RV Parks and Campgrounds.. 85

CHAPTER NINETEEN...**87**

   19. Idaho for Nature Photographers.. 87

   19.1. Scenic Photography Spots... 89

CHAPTER TWENTY..**91**

   20. Idaho's Hidden Gems.. 91

   20.1. Off-the-Beaten-Path Destinations...93

CHAPTER TWENTY-ONE..**95**

   21. Sustainable Travel in Idaho.. 95

   21.1. Ecotourism Initiatives...96

CHAPTER TWENTY-TWO..**98**

   22. Idaho's Arts and Entertainment Scene... 98

   22.1. Galleries and Performing Arts Venues..99

CHAPTER TWENTY-THREE...**102**

   23. Idaho's Native American Heritage... 102

   23.1. Tribal Communities and Cultural Centers....................................... 104

CHAPTER TWENTY-FOUR...**107**

   24. Idaho's Wine and Beer Scene.. 107

   24.1. Wineries and Breweries...108

CHAPTER TWENTY-FIVE...**109**

   25. Idaho's Shopping and Souvenirs.. 109

25.1. Unique Local Products and Markets.. 112

CHAPTER TWENTY-SIX..**114**

26. Idaho's Music Festivals.. 114

26.1. Live Music Events and Festivals.. 118

CHAPTER TWENTY-SEVEN..**120**

27. Idaho's Film and TV Locations... 120

27.1. Famous Filming Locations.. 121

CHAPTER TWENTY-EIGHT..**123**

28. Idaho's Literary Heritage... 123

28.1. Authors and Literary Landmarks.. 124

CHAPTER TWENTY-NINE..**126**

29. Idaho's Technology and Innovation.. 126

29.1. Tech Companies and Research Centers.. 128

CHAPTER-THIRTY...**130**

30. Idaho's Sports Scene.. 130

30.1. Professional and Amateur Sports Teams... 131

CHAPTER-THIRTY ONE...**135**

31. Idaho's LGBTQ+ Friendly Spaces.. 135

31.1. Inclusive Bars and Community Centers... 136

CHAPTER-THIRTY TWO..**138**

32. Idaho's Pet-Friendly Places... 138

32.1. Pet-Friendly Accommodation and Parks.. 142

CHAPTER-THIRTY THREE...**144**

33. Idaho's Volunteer and Community Projects... 144

33.1. Opportunities for Giving Back... 145

CHAPTER THIRTY-FOUR...**147**

34. Idaho's Wellness and Spa Retreats.. 147

34.1. Relaxation and Healing Centers... 148

CHAPTER-THIRTY FIVE...**151**

35. Idaho's Educational and Learning Opportunities... 151

35.1. Workshops and Classes... 152

CHAPTER THIRTY-SIX...**157**

36. Idaho's Religious and Spiritual Sites.. 157

36.1. Churches and Meditation Centers... 158

CHAPTER THIRTY-SEVEN...**160**

37. Idaho's Accessibility and Inclusivity... 160

37.1. Resources for Travelers with Disabilities... 161

CHAPTER THIRTY-EIGHT..**162**

38. Idaho's Emergency Contacts... 162

38.1. Important Phone Numbers and Services.. 163

CHAPTER ONE

1. Introduction to Idaho

From river rafting, to fly fishing, to cruising at 35 miles per hour on fresh powder in search of the tallest sugar tree, indulging in the adrenaline-pumping adventures of skiing and snowmobiling is an absolute must in the scenic wonderland of Idaho! With its breathtaking landscapes and warm hospitality, Idaho proves to be an inviting haven for tourists from all around the world. The people of Idaho take great pride in their state and its rich history, creating an atmosphere that is both welcoming and captivating. And worry not, as Idaho boasts well-maintained roads that effortlessly connect every corner of the state, eliminating any barriers in fulfilling your vacation fantasies. Whether you find euphoria in a 12-ounce elbow flex with a refreshing beverage in hand, or in the vast expanses of the last frontier of the Old American West, Idaho guarantees an unforgettable experience for those who seek the wonders of the great outdoors. With an abundance of whitewater river miles that are just waiting to be explored, world-class fishing destinations that will leave you in awe, numerous prestigious golf courses that cater to every golfer's dream, skiing terrains that offer thrilling descents, and hiking and mountain biking trails that immerse you in the beauty of nature, Idaho truly encompasses the essence of a tourism Mecca for both international adventurers and domestic travelers alike. Despite its countless attractions, the welcoming spirit of Idahoans never wavers, as they wholeheartedly embrace visitors with open arms. Prepare to be amazed as you embark on an unforgettable journey through the enchanting wonders of Idaho!

Idaho isn't always the first state that comes to mind when people imagine the expansive landscape of the American West, but this hidden gem is brimming with endless opportunities to explore and enjoy. From its enchanting lush forests that stretch out as far as the eye can see to the meandering miles of trails that beckon adventurous souls, Idaho truly captivates the hearts of outdoor enthusiasts. The majestic snowy peaked mountains serve as a breathtaking backdrop, adding a touch of awe-inspiring beauty to this remarkable state.

For those seeking thrilling escapades in Idaho's great outdoors, there is an abundance of activities to indulge in. Hiking through the thick forests, you will feel the whisper of ancient trees, as if they are revealing their significant tales to you alone. The trails, adorned with nature's wonders, unveil stunning vistas and hidden treasures at every turn. From cascading waterfalls that create a symphony of nature's melodies to picturesque meadows carpeted with vibrant wildflowers, Idaho's trails are a portal to a world of natural wonders.

Within the delightful towns and cities of Idaho, the less intrepid explorers can also find an array of captivating experiences. Museums brimming with captivating stories and fascinating artifacts await, ready to transport visitors through time and immerse them in the rich history of the region. Marvel at the impressive collections, where every exhibit reveals a tale of Idaho's past, from the native tribes who called this land home to the pioneers who shaped its destiny.

Indulging in the pleasures of Idaho's urban landscapes is equally enchanting. Immerse yourself in the sophisticated elegance of top-of-the-line hotels, where comfort merges seamlessly with impeccable service. Pamper your taste buds in the eclectic array of restaurants, offering a tantalizing array of flavors that range from traditional local cuisine to world-class international delights. With countless delectable options at your disposal, Idaho's culinary scene promises to leave you savoring every bite.

one thing is certain – in Idaho, unforgettable experiences await at every corner, beckoning to create memories that will last a lifetime.

1.1. Geography and Climate

Geography and climate charge the sharpest issues in Idaho. Few places in the United States have more dramatic mountains and canyons or deeper river gorges. In its grandeur, Idaho attracts wide support, but where the land is scarred and poor development occurs, several conservation controversies persist. In one sponsored by a powerful timber industry, traditional drive, the discredited scheme to wrest a large portion of the Idaho wilderness from a heavily opposed state congress became the top issue at Capitol Hill - and it proposed surrounding the pristine Frank Church-River of No Return Wildlands with easy roads to turn these parks into a 'recreation showcase'.

The rich and diverse geography, along with the unique and ever-changing climate, present the sharpest and most pressing issues in the beautiful state of Idaho. With its majestic mountains reaching high into the clouds, its awe-inspiring canyons that seem to stretch for eternity, and its mesmerizing river gorges that delve deep into the earth's core, Idaho truly stands out among all other states in the United States. The sheer magnificence and natural wonder of this state attract countless individuals, drawing wide support and admiration from people all over the world.

However, amidst this grandeur lies a troubling reality. As the land is scarred and poor development practices persist, Idaho finds itself embroiled in several conservation controversies. These contentious debates revolve around the delicate balance between progress and preservation, with stakeholders passionately arguing for their respective interests.

One particular controversy, sponsored by a powerful timber industry, has sparked intense public discourse. It revolves around a traditional drive and a discredited scheme aimed at wresting a large portion of the Idaho wilderness from a heavily opposed state congress. This contentious proposal quickly rose to the forefront of the political agenda at Capitol Hill, capturing widespread attention and raising eyebrows across the nation.

At the heart of this controversial scheme is the plan to encircle the pristine Frank Church-River of No Return Wildlands with easily accessible roads. Proponents of this proposal argue that these roads would transform the untouched wilderness into a dazzling 'recreation showcase,' attracting more visitors and boosting local economies. However, vehement opposition argues that such development would irreversibly scar the natural beauty of the area, risking the delicate ecological balance and threatening the very essence of what makes Idaho's wildlands so precious.

As the conservation debate rages on, Idaho finds itself at a critical crossroads. The clash of interests between those who seek to profit from resource extraction and development and those who champion the preservation of Idaho's natural wonders presents a fundamental question. What is the true value of Idaho's geography and climate? Should they be exploited for short-term gains, or should they be cherished and protected for generations to come?

Only time will tell how this contentious issue unfolds, but one thing is certain – the geography and climate of Idaho will always be at the center of its identity, its allure, and its future. It is a land of untamed beauty, where mountains touch the sky, canyons leave one in awe, and river gorges whisper stories of the earth's history. Idaho's natural wonders are not just a source of pride; they are a reminder of the immense power and beauty that Mother Nature has bestowed upon us. It is our responsibility to safeguard and cherish them, keeping them intact for our children and their children, so that they too may be inspired by the majesty of Idaho's landscapes.

Idaho offers much more than its famed potato reputation may imply. With its jagged alpine peaks piercing the sky, sprawling vistas of golden grain fields and lush potato farms, and breathtaking rivers carving deep canyons through the land, Idaho stands as a truly captivating and picturesque state. Its rugged mountains, rivaling even the majestic peaks of Colorado or Wyoming, and a multitude of regulated rivers add to the charm and allure of this landlocked gem.

Venture into Eastern Idaho, and you'll find yourself amidst vast grasslands adorned with sagebrush, while monumental undulating sand dunes evoke a quintessentially western atmosphere. Truly, Idaho is a pristine and wide open region, brimming with natural wonders waiting to be explored.

1.2. History and Culture

The state of Idaho is not only known for its natural beauty and outdoor activities, but also for its rich history and architectural landmarks. One of the notable attractions in the area is Heise Hot Springs, which is a popular destination for relaxation and rejuvenation. Additionally, the historic Snake River Gorge offers visitors a glimpse into the past, showcasing the rugged and awe-inspiring landscape that has captivated people for centuries.

Boise, the capital city of Idaho, is home to a number of buildings that hold significant historical value. Many of these architectural gems are even listed on the National Register of Historic Places. One such prominent landmark is the historic general prison forward, which stands as a testament to the city's storied past. Another noteworthy site is the Basque Block on Grove Street, a vibrant hub that celebrates the culture and heritage of the Basque people.

Religion also plays a significant role in the city, as evident by the presence of several religious buildings. The Sentmanat House, built in the Tudor style, showcases exquisite craftsmanship and is a sight to behold. St. John's Cathedral and St. Michael's Roman Catholic Cathedral are both cherished places of worship, serving as spiritual sanctuaries for the faithful. These architectural marvels stand as a testament to the devotion and dedication of the community.

Idaho takes great pride in its education system, with a variety of prestigious universities and higher education institutions. Idaho State University, Boise State University, and North Idaho College all provide excellent academic opportunities for students seeking to further their knowledge and skills. Additionally, the University of Idaho houses a renowned health science school, contributing to advancements in research and medical breakthroughs.

For those with a thirst for knowledge, there are various educational exhibits available throughout the state. These exhibits cover a wide range of subjects, including geology, wildlife, and history. Visitors have the opportunity to delve into the fascinating world of these topics, gaining a deeper understanding of Idaho's unique natural features and cultural heritage.

Unlike many other states, Idaho does not rely on privately-run bodies for promotional activities. Instead, a series of voluntary trade organizations take on the responsibility of representing the state and carrying out promotional initiatives. Through their efforts, these organizations strive to showcase the beauty and diversity of Idaho, attracting tourists and promoting economic growth.

In conclusion, Idaho offers a captivating mix of natural wonders, historical landmarks, and educational opportunities. From the stunning Snake River Gorge to the impressive architecture of Boise, there is something for everyone to enjoy in this vibrant state. With its commitment to education and preservation, Idaho continues to thrive as a destination that nourishes both the mind and the spirit.

The state's first inhabitants were various Native American tribes, including the Shoshone, who lived off the land and thrived in harmony with nature. The state's vast landscapes and abundant resources have always attracted explorers and pioneers from different corners of the world. One such explorer was Victorio of Pueblo of Taos, New Mexico, who ventured into Idaho and left a lasting impact on the region's history.

The earliest settlers to call Idaho home were the pioneering Mormons, who arrived in the late 19th century and established the city of Franklin in 1860. These resilient individuals played an integral role in the development of the Snake River Valley, transforming it into an agricultural hub with their innovative farming techniques and unwavering spirit.

However, the story of Idaho's settlement doesn't end with the Mormons. During the gold rush of 1862, a wave of adventurous prospectors flocked to the state in search of fortune and opportunity. They braved treacherous terrains, battling against the elements to fulfill their dreams of striking it rich. The Oregon Trail, a historic pathway that connected the East Coast to the West, also passed through Idaho, leaving a trail of stories and memories that are etched into the fabric of the state's history.

Idaho's rich tapestry of ethnic diversity is yet another fascinating aspect of its past. Over the years, people from various backgrounds and cultures have made Idaho their home, adding their unique flavors to the state's melting pot. Among these diverse communities are the Basque, Chinese, Croatian, Japanese, and Iranian descendants, who have enriched the social and cultural landscape of Idaho.

The Basque people, in particular, hold a significant place in Idaho's narrative. They were the first and largest ethnic group to settle in the area, bringing with them their language, customs, and traditions. Today, they continue to thrive and maintain a strong presence, with their vibrant Basque community being the largest population of Basque outside of their homeland.

Idaho's history is an intricate tapestry woven with the threads of Native American heritage, Mormon pioneers, gold rush adventurers, and waves of immigrants from different corners of the globe. It is a story of resilience, exploration, and the pursuit of dreams. As Idaho continues to evolve, it embraces its past while looking towards a future that promises even greater diversity and progress.

CHAPTER TWO

2. Planning Your Trip

It is indeed possible to embark on a journey to the magnificent state of Idaho by either train or bus, even though it must be noted that the availability of these forms of transportation might be somewhat limited. Fear not, for the Union Pacific Railroad and Amtrak valiantly traverse the wondrous landscapes of Idaho, albeit with a somewhat restricted service. Once you find yourself within the embrace of this great state, worry not about mobility, as car and recreational vehicle rentals can be found in abundance within the larger communities, courtesy of the numerous private rental agencies scattered throughout. Should you require transportation for a large gathering, be informed that chartered bus services are also readily available. Pleasingly, if you opt for the marvelous tour packages thoughtfully curated by Amity Tours and Adventures of Idaho, transportation is already conveniently included. To explore every nook and cranny of Idaho, rest assured that the highways spanning the entirety of the state are impeccably maintained, ensuring a smooth and enjoyable journey. By embarking on this expedition at your own tempo and according to your own preferences, you are sure to immerse yourself in the exceptional allure and grandeur of Idaho, a feeling of tranquility and exultation that simply cannot be replicated elsewhere.

Getting to Idaho from any location is quick and easy because Idaho is conveniently located in the center of the Pacific Northwest. Most major U.S. airlines fly both international and domestic flights into Idaho. Passengers can fly into the Boise or Idaho Falls regional airports or the part-time Lewiston-Nez Perce County Airport. The primary airline in Boise is United, followed by Delta Airlines. In Twin Falls, the main airline is Sky West, and in Pocatello, it is American Airlines. From our regional airports, there are connecting flights to additional communities in Idaho, such as Coeur d'Alene, Sandpoint, Sun Valley, and McCall, offering travelers a wide range of options for reaching their desired destinations in the state. The extensive network of flights ensures that visitors from every corner of the globe can easily access the beautiful landscapes, outdoor activities, and unique cultural experiences that Idaho has to offer. Whether you're coming from the bustling city or a peaceful countryside, Idaho welcomes you with open arms and promises an unforgettable journey filled with spectacular sights and warm hospitality. So pack your bags, book your tickets, and get ready for an adventure like no other in the captivating heart of the Pacific Northwest.

2.1. When to Visit

Idaho continues to remain the place to visit in North America if you are looking to avoid large crowds, immersing yourself in the tranquility that this beautiful state has to offer. Traffic is virtually non-existent any time of the year near the National Parks, allowing you to freely explore and marvel at the untouched natural wonders. The expansive motorhome roads Idaho State creates during the enchanting spring and fall months are some of the most breathtaking and awe-inspiring drives remaining in the United States of America, granting you an unparalleled experience of scenic beauty.

If you can wisely choose to avoid visiting during the bustling summer months, then do so, as the splendors of Idaho truly come alive during the captivating fall season. Witnessing the magnificent transition of the colorful foliage is simply unmatched, a symphony of vibrant hues painting the landscape in a mesmerizing tapestry of gold, red, and orange. As you venture through the captivating terrain, you will find yourself immersed in a world where every turn reveals breathtaking vistas and leaves you awe-inspired.

Moreover, the early springtime search for birds in Idaho is an experience that is hard to beat anywhere in the country. As the wilderness awakens from its wintry slumber, vibrant migratory birds fill the skies, creating a mesmerizing ballet of flight and song. Embark on an unforgettable journey of exploration and discovery, where each new sighting brings a sense of wonder and excitement, offering an opportunity to connect with nature in its purest form.

In conclusion, Idaho beckons those seeking solace and serenity away from the hustle and bustle of crowded tourist destinations. With its secluded National Parks, enchanting motorhome roads, captivating fall colors, and remarkable birdwatching opportunities, Idaho truly embodies the essence of untouched beauty and natural splendor. Embrace the hidden gems that await you in this remarkable state and create memories that will last a lifetime.

Most visitors come to Idaho in the summertime or during the winter months. During summertime, visitors take advantage of Idaho's outdoor opportunities. You will find the most visitors between June and August. Summer is a wonderful season in Idaho, with warm and pleasant weather that allows visitors to fully immerse themselves in the beauty of the state. The summertime landscape in Idaho is a sight to behold, with lush greenery, blooming flowers, and sparkling lakes. It is the perfect time for hiking, camping, fishing, and exploring the numerous national parks and forests that Idaho has to offer. The long daylight hours provide ample time for outdoor adventures and recreational activities, creating unforgettable memories for visitors of all ages.

On the other hand, winter tourism is also quite popular in Idaho, attracting a large number of tourists from January to March. This is the time when the snow blankets the state, creating a winter wonderland that is perfect for winter sports enthusiasts. Idaho's pristine mountains and majestic ski resorts offer some of the best skiing, snowboarding, and snowmobiling experiences in the country. The thrill of gliding down the slopes, surrounded by the stunning snow-covered landscape, is an experience unlike any other. Visitors from all over the world flock to Idaho's winter paradise to enjoy the adrenaline rush of these exhilarating winter activities.

In addition to the summer and winter seasons, spring is gradually gaining popularity among nature lovers and birdwatching enthusiasts. Idaho serves as a vital stopover for various bird species during their migration journey. The state's diverse habitats and ecological wonders attract a wide range of migratory birds, making it a haven for birdwatchers. Springtime in Idaho offers a unique opportunity to witness the awe-inspiring sight of birds in flight, as they traverse the skies above the picturesque landscapes. From colorful songbirds to magnificent raptors, the birdwatching experience in Idaho during the spring season is nothing short of extraordinary. As the days grow longer, the air fills with the beautiful melodies of birdsong, creating a truly enchanting atmosphere for both seasoned birdwatchers and casual enthusiasts.

Whether it's the allure of summer adventures, thrilling winter sports, or the captivating spectacle of spring bird migration, Idaho has something to offer for every type of visitor. With its natural wonders, breathtaking scenery, and an abundance of outdoor activities, it is no wonder that Idaho remains a top destination for travelers throughout the year. So, no matter when you plan to visit, rest assured that Idaho will provide you with an unforgettable experience that will leave you longing to return time and time again.

2.2. Transportation Options

The state's interstates are the East-West Interstate 84 and the North-South Interstates 15 and 95. These interstates, spanning across picturesque landscapes and serving as crucial lifelines for transportation, seamlessly connect to an established network of high-quality multi-lane highways. This extensive web of roads grants effortless accessibility, allowing travelers to explore the charming beauty of Idaho while being within a seven-hour drive time from any city.

Idaho, blessed with low traffic densities and a well-maintained infrastructure, presents an idyllic scenario for commuters. With an average commute time of only 18 minutes, residents can relish in the pleasure of spending more precious moments in the comfort of their homes. This remarkable statistic reflects Idaho's commitment to enhancing the quality of life for its residents, ensuring that they have ample time to enjoy the plentiful amenities the state offers.

Whether it's relishing in the serene tranquility of the breathtaking landscapes, engaging in outdoor adventures, or immersing oneself in the vibrant culture that Idaho embraces, residents here truly have the best of both worlds. The efficient transportation system not only enhances productivity but also fosters a sense of contentment and well-being, as individuals can effortlessly balance work and leisure.

In essence, the transportation infrastructure in Idaho stands as a testament to the state's unwavering dedication to the welfare and satisfaction of its citizens. With a multitude of options for connectivity, Idahoans have the freedom to navigate their lives seamlessly, cherishing the rich experiences within their grasp, and celebrating the extraordinary beauty that their beloved state has to offer. It's an Idaho transportation and productivity fact that brings joy and fulfillment to the lives of its residents every day.

The Clean Air Express, elegantly managed and operated by Americanos U.S.A., stands as a remarkable symbol of efficient transportation for the delighted citizens of the great state of Idaho. This exceptional service gratifies the community with its punctuality and reliability, ensuring a seamless daily journey connecting various picturesque Idaho cities. Passengers are privileged to revel in the panoramic landscapes offered by the vast expanse of Idaho and Eastern Oregon, with the convenience of effortless connections to thriving metropolises within the region. With a commitment to excellence, The Clean Air Express guarantees an extraordinary travel experience, fostering the growth and prosperity of both the local and regional economies.

Idaho is easily accessible by air, train, motor coach, and interstate highways. It is serviced by four major airlines, which offer a wide range of flights to various destinations. The state boasts an extensive transportation network, ensuring convenient travel options for both residents and visitors. The southern part of Idaho is also serviced by the reputable bus company Greyhound, providing reliable transportation for those who prefer bus travel. Additionally, numerous car rental agencies operate throughout the state, offering a diverse selection of vehicles to suit different preferences and needs. Travel within Idaho is made easy with the presence of efficient public transit systems in every city or region, allowing for hassle-free movement and exploration of various attractions. Whether you prefer to fly, take a train, hire a car, or utilize public transportation, Idaho ensures your journey is smooth and efficient.

CHAPTER THREE

3. Top Destinations

The Sawtooth National Forest encompasses well over 2,000,000 acres of magnificent protected and managed lands. This vast and diverse area offers an abundance of outdoor recreational opportunities for nature enthusiasts and adventure seekers alike. Among the more popular attractions that draw the attention of the general traveling public are the wild and scenic Salmon, Payette, and Boise rivers. Along the winding banks of these picturesque waterways, the Forest Service maintains numerous campgrounds, providing a perfect setting for visitors to immerse themselves in the tranquility of nature and create lasting memories.

For those in search of solace and serenity, the forest offers beautiful areas with calmer pools and gentle rapids, ideal for fishing, canoeing, or simply taking a refreshing dip in the crystal-clear waters. One such area that stands out as both iconic and beloved is the breathtaking Redfish Lake. Nestled beside the meandering Redfish Lake Creek, this stunning oasis takes its name from the legendary river that flows from its origins. Redfish Lake is a destination that captivates the hearts of all who visit, providing a myriad of recreational activities to suit every interest.

Camping enthusiasts are in for a treat, as Redfish Lake offers well-appointed camping facilities that blend seamlessly with the surrounding natural beauty. Whether you prefer pitching a tent under the starlit sky or reveling in the comforts of a cozy lodge, there is an option to suit everyone's preferences. Wake up to the gentle lapping of waves against the shore, breathe in the crisp mountain air, and embark on a day of adventure.

Boating enthusiasts will be delighted by the opportunity to explore the shimmering waters of Redfish Lake. Feel the exhilaration as you glide across the surface, surrounded by awe-inspiring vistas of towering mountains and verdant forests. Whether you prefer a leisurely cruise or an adventurous paddle, the lake beckons you to embark on an unforgettable voyage.

For those seeking respite from the summer heat, Redfish Lake offers pristine swimming areas. Immerse yourself in the refreshing waters and let the worries of the world drift away. Happiness and contentment come naturally as you soak up the sun's rays, enveloped by the stunning panorama that surrounds you.

If hiking is your passion, prepare to be captivated by the rugged beauty of the Hidden Lake Trail. This remarkable 5-mile trek is a relatively easy out-and-back journey that meanders through enchanting woodlands and picturesque valleys. Along the way, be prepared to feast your eyes upon breathtaking views of snow-capped mountains and a series of majestic waterfalls. Every step unveils a new marvel of nature, inviting you to pause and capture the moment with your camera.

In conclusion, the Sawtooth National Forest beckons adventurers from near and far, offering a multitude of outdoor experiences in a breathtakingly beautiful setting. Lose yourself in the wonders of nature as you explore the wild and scenic rivers, immerse yourself in the serenity of Redfish Lake, and embark on invigorating hikes that unveil nature's grandeur. Discover the allure of this magnificent forest, where every turn offers a new discovery and every moment is etched into your memory.

Sawtooth National Forest

Centered around the world-renowned Sun Valley Ski Resorts and the breathtaking Sawtooth National Scenic Byway, Sun Valley/Ketchum is an incredibly diverse and captivating destination for all seasons. The immediate Sun Valley/Ketchum area is encompassed by a vast expanse of over 700,000 acres of awe-inspiring protected wilderness, offering an unrivaled opportunity to immerse yourself in the wonders of nature. Among these remarkable landscapes are the stunning Sawtooth, Hemingway-Bouldering, and White Cloud Wilderness Areas, located within the renowned Sawtooth National Recreation Area. Additionally, the extraordinary Sawtooth, Cecil D. Andrus-White Clouds, and Jim McClure-Jerry Peak Wildernesses are found within the expansive Sawtooth National Forest. These expansive wilderness areas perfectly complement the majestic 2.35 million-acre Frank Church-River of No Return Wilderness, which proudly holds the distinction of being the largest wilderness area in the contiguous United States. To fully grasp the magnitude of these extraordinary environments, one must witness them firsthand - they are truly a sight to behold. If you are yearning to delve into the untamed beauty of this country, look no further than Sun Valley/Ketchum, as it plays host to a multitude of experienced and knowledgeable professional wilderness guides. Within a mere hour's drive from Sun Valley, you will find yourself transcending into a world untouched by the mundane, leaving your car and worries behind. Before long, you'll be serenely watching as your fly gracefully dances upon the pristine waters of countless picturesque mountain lakes, a testament to the enchanting allure of this remarkable region.

Sun Valley/Sawtooth National Recreation Area is a stunning destination that offers breathtaking natural landscapes and recreational activities for all nature enthusiasts. Located in the heart of Idaho, this vast area is a wilderness paradise, encompassing the magnificent Frank Church-River of No Return Wilderness.

The Sun Valley/Sawtooth National Recreation Area is an outdoor haven, boasting diverse ecosystems, including alpine meadows, dense forests, crystal-clear lakes, and towering mountain peaks. With ample opportunities for hiking, camping, fishing, wildlife watching, and winter sports, this area caters to adventure seekers and tranquility seekers alike.

The Frank Church-River of No Return Wilderness, named after the renowned senator Frank Church, is one of the largest designated wilderness areas in the United States. Spanning an impressive expanse, this wilderness area is a sanctuary for nature preservation, allowing visitors to experience the awe-inspiring beauty of untouched landscapes.

While exploring the Sun Valley/Sawtooth National Recreation Area and the Frank Church-River of No Return Wilderness, you can embark on scenic hikes that lead you through picturesque trails and offer breathtaking views at every turn. The abundance of wildlife, including elk, deer, wolves, and many bird species, adds an element of intrigue to your adventure.

For those seeking a thrilling experience, the area provides opportunities for rock climbing, whitewater rafting, horseback riding, and mountain biking. When winter blankets the region, it transforms into a snowy wonderland, inviting visitors to indulge in activities such as skiing, snowboarding, snowshoeing, and snowmobiling.

To fully appreciate the beauty of nature in this remarkable region, take a leisurely boat ride on the pristine lakes, bask in the serenity of the surroundings, and immerse yourself in the tranquility of the wilderness.

The Sun Valley/Sawtooth National Recreation Area and the Frank Church-River of No Return Wilderness truly offer an escape from the hustle and bustle of everyday life. With its unparalleled natural wonders and endless opportunities for adventure, this destination promises an unforgettable experience that will leave you in awe of the magnificence of the great outdoors.

3.1. Boise

Though the Cascade still rolls the dice, temperatures cool down into the 50s and 60s. In the winter months, travelers can expect it to frequently go below freezing, but to rarely stay there for an extended period of time. Boise's coldest month is January, which averages a crisp, dry 31°F during the day and a likeable, sleep-under-the-quilts 21°F during the darker, colder nights. The city is well-known for its long, relatively frost-free springs and autumns, but as many dry air masses and wet air masses pass over the city during the transitional seasons, the weather can be rather variable and unpredictable. Snowfall is infrequent, typically only occurring during storm periods, and in an average winter season, it amounts to a modest 19.5 inches a year. However, it's worth noting that snow cover doesn't last for an extended period of time either, with bare ground usually reappearing shortly after the sky has cleared. Thankfully, as the days grow longer and the temperatures gradually rise, the sun will return to breathe life into the Boise River and its picturesque Bike Trail. It will also attract new music and vibrant energy into the city, as well as coax the flowers out of their deep winter and early-spring hibernation period, painting the landscape with splashes of color.

Upon arriving in Boise, one can be forgiven for thinking they have fallen into a city of old that has recently been modernized. The Boise River, with its tranquil flow, gracefully meanders through the heart of the city, whispering secrets of its timeless presence to all those who listen. It declares, "I've been here for centuries, faithfully serving the land, but that doesn't mean I cannot bestow upon your city a touch of enchantment." As you explore the city's riverfront, you will witness a harmonious unity forged over time, where the buildings rise alongside the waters with a refined elegance. Unlike the soaring concrete giants of other metropolitan areas, these historic structures proudly showcase their roots in the region's local craftsmanship. Each brick carries the weight of nostalgia, exuding the essence of a bygone era that tantalizes the senses. They beckon, whispering, "if you seek significance, I am your cornerstone, your essential foundation."

Strolling through the streets, one cannot help but admire the intricate details woven into the tapestry of Boise's architectural heritage. The old brick leaves its mark in delicate trims, steadfast footings, resilient foundations, and majestic lintels. It is a testament to the artistry and enduring spirit that unites past and present, allowing glass and steel to speak only the language of necessity, rather than the verbose symphony of towering skyscrapers synonymous with cities like Chicago, New York, Boston, or Philadelphia. In Boise, the buildings converse with both reverence and restraint, whispering stories of their own without overshadowing the tranquil majesty of the natural surroundings. As you navigate the city's timeless streets, the idyllic blend of old-world charm and subtle modernity leaves an indelible impression on your soul, forever intertwining your journey with the rich tapestry of Boise's history.

3.2. Sun Valley

Sun Valley, known for its mesmerizing beauty and unparalleled offerings, warmly welcomes visitors from Thanksgiving, all the way until the glorious arrival of Easter. The peak ski seasons witness an influx of avid skiers and snowboarders, with their numbers soaring to an astounding count of around 30,000. But that's not all - Sun Valley's allure extends beyond the snowy wonderland, as even during the summer months, this captivating destination transforms into a playground for passionate golfers and tennis aficionados alike.

Unveiling a world of sophistication, Sun Valley boasts an array of amenities and facilities that are designed to cater to every discerning visitor. It seamlessly caters to the needs of the sports-minded, high-speed vacationers, as well as captivates the hearts of those seeking a more leisurely retreat. Whether you seek thrilling adventures on the slopes or yearn to simply unwind and bask in the enchantment of America's most renowned resort area, Sun Valley warmly embraces all who cross its path, promising an experience that will forever be etched in your memories.

Sun Valley, known for its world-class alpine skiing, is both a stunningly beautiful and exciting vacation resort area nestled in the heart of the magnificent mountains. The Sun Valley Lodge, renowned for its luxurious accommodations and exceptional hospitality, stands tall as the beacon of elegance and charm, enchanting visitors from all corners of the globe. However, beyond the grandeur of the lodge, lies an enchanting array of attractions and activities, designed to captivate and thrill every traveler who steps foot in this haven of boundless possibilities.

For those with a penchant for the arts, Sun Valley offers an abundance of cultural experiences that will ignite the senses and nurture the soul. Immerse yourself in the hypnotic melodies of live music performances that resonate through the valleys, as talented musicians breathe life into their instruments. Delve into the world of theatrical wonders at the local playhouses, where captivating performances transport you to realms of imagination and emotion. Explore the eclectic art galleries adorned with masterpieces that embody the essence of creativity and inspire the mind.

Adrenaline seekers will find their sanctuary amidst the rugged landscapes of Sun Valley. Saddle up and embark on an exhilarating horseback riding adventure, galloping through picturesque trails that wind through meadows and forests. For the daring souls ready to embrace a true wild west experience, witness the heart-pounding spectacle of team bronco busting, where courageous cowboys tame untamed spirits with unparalleled skill and bravery. Feel the rush as you witness the thunderous hooves and witness the harmonious bond between man and beast.

Nature lovers will find solace in Sun Valley's breathtaking surroundings. Discover hidden treasures as you embark on scenic hikes that lead to majestic waterfalls, unveiling nature's pristine beauty at every turn. Immerse yourself in the serenity of fishing, as you cast your line into tranquil rivers, feeling the anticipation build as you wait for a gentle tug. Lose yourself in the vastness of the mountains as you partake in thrilling mountain biking expeditions, conquering terrain that challenges even the most fearless adventurers.

With each passing moment, Sun Valley reveals another facet of its multifaceted allure, leaving an indelible mark on the hearts of those who dare to explore its wonders. Whether it's the snow-capped peaks that glisten in the winter sun or the vibrant colors that adorn the landscape during warmer months, this extraordinary destination promises a truly unforgettable experience for all who seek adventure, beauty, and the joy of discovery. Embark on a journey to Sun Valley and let your imagination roam free in this extraordinary playground of possibilities.

3.3. Coeur d'Alene

The North Idaho Centennial Trail (nonmotorized) is a picturesque route that spans an impressive 24 miles, stretching from the scenic Idaho/Washington state line near Post Falls to the unparalleled beauty of the village of Harrison at the southern tip of the magnificent lake. With great dedication and collaboration, this trail was brought to life, thanks to the tireless efforts of the esteemed Coeur d'Alene Resort Association. As you traverse this trail, you will be captivated by the awe-inspiring landscapes it takes you through, guiding you along various parks, the serene lakefront, and the majestic Spokane River. One of the most incredible aspects of this trail is the abundance of access points it offers, allowing you to fully immerse yourself in a wide array of recreational opportunities.

Coeur d'Alene, renowned for its lakeside charm, is a destination that boasts an array of attractions that are sure to capture your heart. At the heart of it all is the iconic Coeur d'Alene Resort, a true gem that has become synonymous with luxury and elegance. This extraordinary resort is home to a world-class convention facility, which is not only grand in size but also offers a comprehensive range of services to meet your every need. As you explore the resort, don't forget to visit its remarkable full-service marina, where you can delight in a seamless blend of opulent amenities and the tranquility of the surrounding lake.

Every year, the region celebrates its rich heritage through the highly anticipated annual Wooden Boat Show. This cherished event serves as a testament to the deep-rooted history of north Idaho while showcasing the remarkable craftsmanship and ingenuity associated with wooden boats. With each boat on display, you can witness the remarkable connection between the captivating lake surroundings and the pure joy of boating. This harmonious bond truly reflects the spirit of the city and the lake, capturing the essence of their unique character.

Embark on the North Idaho Centennial Trail and experience the harmonious symphony of nature's finest offerings intertwined with the rich history and cultural tapestry of this remarkable region. Whether you seek adventure, serenity, or a delightful combination of both, this trail is sure to leave an indelible mark on your heart and soul.

Coeur d'Alene is a city located in the picturesque Idaho panhandle, renowned for its charming beauty and thriving community. With an impressive population of over 45,000 residents, this vibrant city stands as a testament to the rich history and cultural heritage it possesses. Known affectionately by the native tribes as Schitsu'umsh, which translates to "place of the discovered arrow," Coeur d'Alene holds a profound significance in the hearts of those who call it home.

Steeped in a captivating past, the roots of Coeur d'Alene trace back to the early 19th century when fur traders first ventured into this bountiful region in 1812. However, it was not until 1842 that Catholic missionaries established a mission here, only to have it temporarily closed due to the eruption of Indian hostilities. Undeterred by the challenges, the mission was reestablished in 1877, symbolizing the resilience and enduring spirit of the people.

Nowadays, Coeur d'Alene is a thriving tourist destination, attracting a multitude of visitors craving unforgettable experiences and breathtaking adventures. One of its main draws lies in the plethora of recreational activities available, catering to a wide range of interests. Enthusiastic boaters, avid fishermen, and passionate sailors flock to the crystal-clear waters of the area, indulging in their beloved pursuits amidst a picturesque backdrop. For those with a penchant for the great outdoors, Coeur d'Alene offers an extensive network of hiking trails, inviting explorers to immerse themselves in the awe-inspiring beauty of nature.

Golf enthusiasts from near and far are captivated by the allure of Coeur d'Alene's world-renowned golf courses. Featuring an array of top-ranked greens, golfers are treated to an unforgettable experience, their swings gracefully guiding them through fairways kissed by gentle breezes. Among these prestigious courses, the Coeur d'Alene Resort's floating green stands as an iconic testament to the city's commitment to providing a truly exceptional golfing experience.

Venturing into the downtown waterfront area reveals a remarkable transformation that has taken place in recent years, thanks to the dedicated efforts of the Urban Renewal District. Thriving with renewed vitality, this bustling district has become a beloved hub for residents and visitors alike. Art lovers can explore enchanting art galleries, where vibrant colors and captivating masterpieces adorn the walls, while antique enthusiasts can peruse the charming stores, diligently searching for hidden treasures. Sidewalk cafes exude an inviting ambiance, offering indulgent culinary delights, while the gentle lapping of waves and the refreshing scent of the lake beckon tourists to enjoy leisurely strolls along the shoreline.

Coeur d'Alene's namesake lake stands as a captivating centerpiece, infusing the city with a sense of tranquility and natural beauty. Its shimmering waters mirror the surrounding landscape, painting a mesmerizing tableau that is sure to captivate the hearts of all who encounter it. As the sun sets gracefully on the horizon, casting vibrant hues across the sky, the city of Coeur d'Alene radiates with a timeless charm that words can scarcely capture.

In conclusion, Coeur d'Alene is a captivating city nestled in the Idaho panhandle, offering a wealth of treasures to discover. From its fascinating history to its abundant recreational opportunities and thriving downtown district, this remarkable city has something for everyone. Whether you seek adventure, tranquility, or a vibrant cultural experience, Coeur d'Alene stands ready to embrace you with open arms, leaving an indelible mark on your heart and memories that will last a lifetime.

CHAPTER FOUR

4. Outdoor Activities

Almost one-fourth of the nation's trout resources are found in Idaho, making it a haven for fishing enthusiasts. The state boasts abundant opportunities for sport fishing, with each season bringing its own unique charm. Idaho is home to an impressive variety of fish species, with over 50 being found in its 2,000 lakes and 18,000 miles of waterways. These pristine ecosystems also support a diverse range of wildlife, including forest grouse and mourning doves.

Nature lovers flock to Idaho due to its reputation as a wildlife paradise. One particularly captivating sight for wildlife watchers is the natural hotspot in the Payette National Forest, where moose and elk can be spotted throughout the year. This phenomenon offers a rare opportunity to observe these majestic creatures up close and personal.

In addition to its captivating wildlife, privately owned properties in Idaho provide incredible bird-watching opportunities. Throughout the year, various species of birds grace the fields, including hawks, goldfinches, purple Martins, and other melodious songbirds. Moreover, the field is not the only place to spot avian wonders. Trumpeter swans, wood ducks, northern shovelers, Canada geese, and blue-winged teal are known to visit feeders in McCall or seek refuge in the protected reserve of Marysville.

Idaho's vast expanse of wilderness and the wide range of activities it offers can be overwhelming when deciding where to explore. Whether you prefer hiking through pristine forests, fishing in tranquil lakes, or observing the abundance of wildlife, Idaho has something for everyone's taste. It's not a question of finding something to do but rather choosing where to embark on your next adventure.

If you haven't noticed yet, the whole of Idaho is considered to be pristine wilderness, so outdoor activities are second-nature here. There are miles and miles of trails for hiking and backpacking, providing endless opportunities to immerse yourself in nature's splendor and discover hidden gems along the way. Moreover, thousands of miles of waterways await, inviting you to embark on thrilling rafting adventures or leisurely floats, as you traverse the stunning landscapes and bask in the tranquility that surrounds you.

What makes Idaho truly exceptional is that more than half the state's land is public land, opening up abundant possibilities for exploration and recreation. With such vast expanses at your disposal, accessing these natural wonders is a breeze. As you venture into the wilderness, you'll find yourself captivated by the diverse ecosystems that thrive here, marveling at the untouched beauty that stretches as far as the eye can see.

Among the countless remarkable excursions available in Idaho, one stands out as an absolute favorite: the Middle Fork of the Salmon River. Spanning an impressive distance of 100 miles, this iconic river journey promises an unforgettable experience filled with captivating sights and exhilarating encounters with wildlife. As you navigate its shimmering rapids, you'll feel a surge of adrenaline coursing through your veins. And when you stumble upon the soothing hot springs that dot the landscape, you'll understand why this adventure holds such allure. Whether it be the rush of adrenaline or the chance to immerse yourself in nature's embrace, the Middle Fork of the Salmon River offers a truly extraordinary expedition for all who dare to venture here.

Moreover, Idaho boasts another exceptional river system that has gained widespread acclaim, thanks to the truly remarkable Olympic whitewater events: the Lochsa River System. Set amidst breathtaking scenery, as soon as your fingertips graze the surface of these roiling sapphire waters, you'll be instantly enchanted. Many enthusiasts and nature-lovers regard the Lochsa River System as the crown jewel of the Northwest rivers, and it's not hard to see why. When April, May, and June roll around, the white water roars with intensity, offering an adrenaline-pumping experience like no other, with rapids rushing past at a staggering speed of 20 minutes per mile. However, if you prefer a more serene outing, fear not. At other times of the year, the Lochsa River System unveils a more peaceful demeanor, perfect for those seeking a gentler adventure. Fishing enthusiasts can cast their lines into the calm waters, eager to reel in the abundant fish that call this river home. If floating leisurely is more to your liking, then you'll relish in the opportunity to drift along effortlessly, soaking in the picturesque surroundings that seem almost too beautiful to be real.

4.1. Hiking and Camping

4.1.1. Maps: The Federation of Western Outdoor Clubs, an esteemed organization dedicated to outdoor exploration and adventure, takes pride in providing a plethora of meticulously crafted maps that span across the enchanting Pacific Northwest region. For the picturesque state of Idaho, they offer a delightful array of maps that capture the essence of its natural splendor. Among these exquisite offerings, their Sawtooth and White Cloud Mountains map will transport you to majestic peaks and serene valleys, while their City of Rocks map will guide you through astounding rock formations that seem to defy gravity. Additionally, their Magruder CIA map offers an intricate exploration of captivating landscapes, while the Gospel Hump/Frank Church River of No Return map captures the essence of untouched wilderness.

In addition to the Federation's commendable efforts, it is highly recommended to explore the remarkable maps issued by the esteemed United States Geological Survey (USGS) and the United States Government Printing Office (USGPO). These exceptional publications can be conveniently ordered from any USGS office, ensuring easy access to a wealth of geographic information. These maps, born out of careful research and expertise, hold the power to transport you to the heart of historical expeditions and assist in retracing the steps of intrepid explorers.

While these renowned cartographic resources provide an exceptional foundation, it is worth noting that there are other remarkable maps available in the area, waiting to be discovered.

These local gems, often priced at a reasonable $6, offer coverage of intriguing regions, complete with expertly documented signed-in routes and detailed road access information. By acquiring these maps, you open the door to hidden treasures and embark on unforgettable adventures.

When venturing through the charming mountain towns of Idaho, you will be delighted to stumble upon a myriad of specialized maps tailored to the unique characteristics of each locale. These distinctive maps, particularly those referenced in section 4.1.8, hold the key to unraveling the secrets of the land. They are a testament to the ongoing dedication and passion of those who have explored Idaho extensively. Furthermore, for those venturing into the enchanting landscapes of Idaho for the first time, the trail guides available are an invaluable resource, providing comprehensive information and serving as trusted companions throughout the journey.

In conclusion, the Federation of Western Outdoor Clubs, in collaboration with the USGS, USGPO, and local enthusiasts, offers a rich tapestry of maps that cater to the desires of intrepid explorers. Whether you seek to conquer soaring mountains, marvel at unique rock formations, or lose yourself in the untamed wilderness, these maps will serve as your guiding light, leading you towards unforgettable experiences and creating cherished memories that will last a lifetime.

Because of its ruggedness and vast natural beauty, many areas in Idaho are best experienced through adventurous hikes, allowing explorers to truly immerse themselves in the stunning surroundings. Like many destinations around the world, the most exceptional regions are often those carefully preserved as federal lands, including the magnificent national forests, awe-inspiring national parks, and particularly in Idaho, the breathtaking Salmon River and Gospel Hump Primitive Areas. These protected areas exude a sense of untouched wilderness, beckoning hikers to embark on remarkable journeys of discovery.

It is worth noting that although southern central Idaho lacks a prominent mountain range, it is home to an exceptional hiking area known as the City of Rocks. This remarkable location, nestled near the convergence of the California and Oregon trails in the enchanting Magic Valley, lures adventurers with its unique rock formations and historical significance. The City of Rocks offers a captivating blend of extraordinary geological wonders and rich cultural heritage, making it an unforgettable destination for hikers and history enthusiasts alike.

In addition to its remarkable landscapes, Idaho boasts an abundance of campgrounds that cater to both the adventurous spirit and the yearning for tranquility. With both primitive and improved campgrounds, a haven awaits every nature lover. These carefully curated sites provide an opportunity to reconnect with the great outdoors, offering a range of facilities and amenities that enhance the camping experience. Moreover, for those seeking a touch of modern comfort, a multitude of RV parks are scattered throughout the state, welcoming travelers with open arms. These convenient and well-appointed havens allow visitors to combine the joy of outdoor exploration with the comforts of home on wheels.

Furthermore, Idaho is graced with numerous summer homes, nestled in idyllic locations throughout the state. These charming retreats provide a sanctuary for those seeking respite from the demands of everyday life. Surrounded by the sublime beauty of Idaho's landscapes, these summer homes offer a serene escape, allowing residents and visitors alike to bask in the tranquility of their surroundings. From cozy cabins nestled amidst towering pines to lakeside retreats basking in the golden sunlight, each summer home possesses its own unique charm, creating an enticing tapestry of relaxation options in Idaho's natural paradise.

Idaho's dedication to preserving its natural wonders, coupled with the abundance of opportunities for hiking, camping, and retreat, makes it a haven for outdoor enthusiasts. Whether embarking on an invigorating hike through untamed wilderness, setting up camp under a canopy of stars, or finding solace in a quaint summer home, Idaho offers a myriad of choices to satisfy the wanderlust of every soul. Come and discover the magic that lies within this rugged gem of the American West.

4.2. Skiing and Snowboarding

Regarded as the "crown jewel of skiing in the west," Sun Valley is home to not just one, but two of the oldest and most iconic ski areas in America. These majestic mountains, known as Mountains B and C, have played a significant role in shaping the world of skiing as we know it today.

But what truly sets Sun Valley apart from other ski destinations is its rich history. It was right here, amidst the breathtaking beauty of this snow-covered paradise, that the very first chairlift in the world was erected. This groundbreaking invention revolutionized the sport, making it accessible to all and transforming the way people experienced the mountains.

Today, Mountains B and C stand proudly as the on- and off-loading points for a true marvel of engineering - the world's first detachable quad chairlift. This remarkable innovation allows skiers and snowboarders to ascend to the heights of the mountains with ease and descend with exhilaration, all while enjoying unmatched comfort and convenience.

But the wonders of Sun Valley don't end there. For those seeking a more adventurous experience, the wilderness backcountry tours from both Bald and Dollar Mountains offer a thrilling escape. Catering to skiers of all levels, these tours provide an opportunity to explore the untouched beauty of the wild terrain and feel a sense of freedom like never before.

Sun Valley is also a haven for specialty skiing experiences that cater to the most avid thrill-seekers. From alpine skiing to antarctic skiing, carving to freestyle, and even snowcat or heli-skiing, there is something to satisfy every adrenaline junkie's heart's desire. For those looking to push the boundaries even further, Sun Valley offers the thrill of snow kiting, a mesmerizing sport that combines the exhilaration of skiing with the power of the wind.

For those with a taste for the truly extreme, Sun Valley presents opportunities for ski-mountaineering and mountaineering, where brave souls can conquer the most formidable peaks. But perhaps the most heart-racing and awe-inspiring of them all is the adrenaline-pumping adventure of extreme skiing. This is where the real daredevils test their mettle, sliding down unnavigated slopes at high speeds, pushing the limits in inaccessible areas, and conquering cliffs, boulders, and even trees with unimaginable skill and precision.

Sun Valley is so much more than just a ski destination - it is a haven for those who seek the thrill of the mountains, the breathtaking beauty of untouched snow, and the unparalleled adrenaline rush that comes from conquering the most challenging slopes. With its rich history, diverse terrain, and endless adventures, Sun Valley truly deserves its title as the crown jewel of skiing in the west.

Skiing and snowboarding. Whether you want to blaze down groomed trails, plow through untracked powder, or launch off of a rail, a fun-filled day of alpine skiing or snowboarding will provide you with hours of exhilarating outdoor entertainment. Explore the vast wonders of the ski resorts in Idaho, where you are greeted with a staggering joint total of 9,600 skiable acres, 293 lifts, and the awe-inspiring longest continuous powder run in North America spanning an impressive distance of 3.1 miles. Embark on an unforgettable adventure at Snow King Mountain, nestled in the heart of Wyoming, which proudly boasts the remarkable title of "The Last Real Mountain Town."

Not only does skiing and snowboarding offer thrilling competition and exciting chairlift rides, but it also presents an array of other captivating options. Perhaps you seek a more intimate connection with nature and desire to revel in the tranquility of cross-country skiing. Immerse yourself in the serenity of over 3,500 miles of meticulously groomed or tracked trails spread across seven breathtaking Nordic areas. For those seeking a challenge and a fantastic cardiovascular workout, dare to engage in the invigorating motion of telemark skiing—a harmonious blend of uphill and downhill maneuvers that will leave you feeling both accomplished and invigorated.

Regardless of your chosen pursuit, the world of skiing and snowboarding beckons with boundless possibilities. From the adrenaline rush of descending groomed slopes to the thrill of conquering untouched powder, each moment spent on the slopes guarantees an enthralling experience. So gear up, embrace the winter wonderland, and let the mountains become your playground as you embark on an enchanting journey through the captivating realms of alpine sports.

CHAPTER FIVE

5. Wildlife and Nature

Idaho is home to an extensive range of breathtakingly beautiful natural scenery, vast farmland, and an astounding array of diverse animal wildlife that will leave you in awe. Prepare to be captivated as you delve deeper into Idaho's abundant natural beauty in this meticulously detailed section of the guide! Firstly, let's marvel at the majestic towering forested mountain ranges that paint the horizon, accompanied by lush, verdant grassy hills that stretch as far as the eye can see. As if that wasn't enough, Idaho also bestows upon us its wondrous deserts, each with its own unique charm and mystique.

When you witness Idaho's natural beauty firsthand, you'll quickly come to realize that it operates on an unprecedented scale of magnificence. The awe-inspiring changes in elevation across the state give rise to an astonishingly diverse set of animal wildlife, transforming every journey through Idaho into an extraordinary encounter with nature. In fact, Idaho boasts an impressive six national wildlife refuges, each an invaluable sanctuary for countless species of awe-inspiring animals. But that's not all – brace yourself for an extraordinary revelation: two of Idaho's majestic forests have been designated as a US president's national park.

Let us venture into the remarkable realm of the Salmon-Challis national forest, where you'll discover the awe-inspiring Craters of the Moon National Monument. Prepare to be astounded by the sight of 1,000-degree blue lava rock, which undergoes an astonishing transformation, showcasing mesmerizing hues of white, yellow, and red, all due to the captivating presence of sulfur. The wonders of this geological marvel will leave you utterly spellbound.

But the wonders of Idaho's natural beauty do not cease there – prepare to be entranced by the breathtakingly picturesque Sawtooth National Recreation Area. This enchanting oasis boasts the ruggedly beautiful Jagged Sawtooth Mountains, whose majestic peaks pierce the heavens, while rolling grasslands gently sway in harmonious rhythm below. And what would a paradise be without crystal clear alpine lakes exuding serenity and tranquility? Here in the Sawtooth National Recreation Area, you're invited to immerse yourself in the pristine waters, a profound experience that will rejuvenate your spirit.

As we traverse the scenic byways of Idaho, we embark on a mesmerizing journey that transports us to captivating scenic views that exceed all expectations. Brace yourself for the incomparable grandeur of Shoshone Falls, a magnificent waterfall that will leave you breathless with its sheer magnitude. And if that's not enough, the Mesa Falls Scenic Byway awaits, a pathway to yet another extraordinary marvel provided by Idaho's astonishing landscape. Prepare to be awestruck as you feast your eyes upon the sublime beauty of Mesa Falls, a thunderous cascade that tumbles with fierce grace, leaving an indelible impression on your very soul.

Indeed, Idaho's natural beauty knows no bounds, with each corner of this magnificent state offering a unique and awe-inspiring experience. From towering mountains and rolling hills to stunning deserts and crystal-clear lakes, Idaho is a haven for those seeking solace in nature's embrace. Discover the wonders that await you in this enchanting land, where every step brings you closer to the captivating harmony of the great outdoors.

5.1. National Parks and Wildlife Refuges

Yellowstone National Park is globally renowned for its breathtaking and awe-inspiring geysers, hot springs, and other remarkable geothermal features, which present an extraordinary and unparalleled avenue for exploration. Nestled within an easily accessible distance, the illustrious caldera of the once formidable and fearsome volcano, combined with the sheer magnificence of Yellowstone, is conveniently located just a mere hour and a half drive away from the vibrant communities of Idaho Falls, Twin Falls, and other bustling Idaho locales. Offering an extensive array of captivating activities throughout the seasons, Yellowstone caters to diverse interests, making it an exquisite and captivating destination throughout the entire year. During the winter months, adrenaline-seekers can indulge in exhilarating snowmobile tours, tranquil cross country skiing escapades, and riveting snowcoach tours, providing an opportunity to embrace the serene and peaceful ambiance enveloping the park. Conversely, the summer season ushers in a multitude of delights, including invigorating hiking excursions, engaging guided tours led by knowledgeable experts, and serene camping experiences immersed in the unrivaled natural setting. Truly, Yellowstone National Park stands as a testament to the unparalleled beauty that nature has to offer, beckoning visitors with open arms to immerse themselves in its awe-inspiring wonders.

In Idaho, guests may find an abundance of national parks, monuments, wildlife refuges, and popular state parks at nearly every corner of this breathtaking state. It is indeed a paradise for nature enthusiasts, as over 60 percent of the world-famous and awe-inspiring Yellowstone National Park is nestled within the geographic boundaries of Idaho. When visiting this natural wonder, one can immerse themselves in its beauty and unparalleled wonders, starting with the central visitor center located in the charming town of Mammoth, which welcomes visitors through the north entrance.

For those seeking further exploration, the stunning Grand Teton National Park awaits just a few miles southeast of Idaho on the picturesque west side of the majestic Teton Range. Prepare to be mesmerized by its towering peaks, serene lakes, and abundant wildlife, all nestled within this remarkable treasure of nature.

As travelers venture southeast, they will discover a myriad of captivating destinations, each offering its own unique charm and experiences. The Sawtooth Mountains beckon with their rugged beauty, inviting hikers and outdoor enthusiasts to explore their majestic trails. Craters of the Moon, with its otherworldly volcanic landscapes, provides a striking contrast to the surrounding areas, offering a glimpse into the Earth's fascinating geological history. History buffs and adventurers alike will find themselves captivated by the City of Rocks, where towering granite formations and hidden caves transport visitors to another time and place.

Don't miss the opportunity to visit Hagerman Fossil Beds National Monument, a testament to Idaho's rich paleontological heritage. Here, one can marvel at the remarkably preserved fossils, which tell the stories of prehistoric creatures and ancient ecosystems that once thrived in this region.

While exploring the wonders of Idaho, take a moment to visit Arco, home to the world's first Atomic Energy Laboratory. Immerse yourself in its intriguing history and learn about the groundbreaking advancements in atomic energy that have shaped our world. Today, this historic landmark is part of the National Atomic Museum, offering visitors a fascinating glimpse into the scientific achievements of the past.

For those seeking a tranquil retreat amidst nature, a wildlife refuge in the picturesque Upper Snake River Valley awaits near the vibrant city of Idaho Falls. Here, one can immerse themselves in the serene surroundings, spot a plethora of wildlife, and experience the tranquility that only the great outdoors can provide.

In Idaho, the possibilities are endless, and the natural wonders seem to be never-ending. Whether one is seeking adventure, tranquility, or simply a deeper connection with nature, this extraordinary state promises to surpass all expectations. Embark on an unforgettable journey through Idaho's national parks, monuments, wildlife refuges, and state parks, and prepare to be amazed at every turn. The beauty of this remarkable state is simply unparalleled, and its treasures are beckoning you to explore, discover, and be inspired.

CHAPTER SIX

6. Idaho's Culinary Scene

Corn, wheat, potato, and other roots are abundantly grown and harvested in the beautiful state of Idaho. This region is renowned for its fertile land, which also yields an impressive array of crops such as sugar beets, barley, and a variety of specialty crops. Among these, hops for brewing thrive, enhancing the craft beer culture, while the orchards produce peaches that are perfectly ripe for picking. Furthermore, the vast countryside of Idaho is adorned with sprawling vineyards, their acres expanding as far as the eye can see.

When it comes to experiencing the culinary wonders of Idaho, one cannot help but seek out locally-produced products. From the rich soil to the talented hands that cultivate it, Idaho prides itself on delivering flavors that are unmatched in their freshness and quality. Immerse yourself in the essence of this exceptional region and raise a glass of Idaho wine or beer in a toast to its incredible terroir.

While exploring Idaho's vibrant culinary scene, the options are endless. Indulge your taste buds at the city's popular revolving restaurants, where every bite is a testament to innovation and flavor. Alternatively, venture off the beaten path and discover the hidden gems that showcase Idaho's lesser-known culinary delights. In the midst of this gastronomic paradise, one thing remains constant: a celebration of the rich heritage and success stories of the pioneering families and farmers who have helped shape Idaho's culinary landscape.

Embark on a culinary adventure that will awaken your senses and transport you to the heart of Idaho's bountiful offerings. From farm to fork, the journey is imbued with passion, dedication, and an unwavering commitment to preserving the traditions that have made Idaho's cuisine so extraordinary. So, whether you find yourself savoring a delectable meal at a bustling eatery or unearthing a hidden treasure tucked away in the countryside, embrace the culinary wonders of Idaho and become part of its enduring legacy.

Idaho has an incredible agricultural bounty that has significantly contributed to the flourishing culinary scene in the region. In this vibrant gastronomic landscape, you will find a multitude of innovative chefs, exceptionally skilled artisans, and visionary individuals who have capitalized on the abundance of locally grown ingredients. Prepare to embark on a delectable journey, as you tantalize your taste buds with the fruits of Idaho farmers' labor, showcased through seasonally-inspired cuisine crafted with the state's freshest produce, locally raised meats that are second to none, and a delightful array of handcrafted beverages. Idaho boasts an impressive array of dining options, catering to every preference and palate. Prepare to be amazed as you uncover nationally renowned restaurants, brimming with talented culinary maestros, hidden within the charming confines of Idaho's many unique towns. Traverse the culinary landscape and discover hidden gems, where locally-sourced ingredients are transformed into exquisite dishes, creating an unparalleled dining experience in the heart of Idaho.

6.1. Local Cuisine and Food Festivals

Festivals and fairs help everyone find something to celebrate, whether it be the opening of ski season (as in Sun Valley), the Snake River Stampede (last year won the naming rights to the Top Large Outdoor Rodeo of the Year by the Professional Rodeo Cowboys Association for the 14th time), a Celtic festival, or any of the approximately 20 annual dog-friendly festivals. Over ten food festivals occur each year as many varieties of apples are celebrated as well as huckleberries. People come to compete in the national Dutch oven Cook-off. Dine from haute cuisine to county fair corn dogs, burgers, and fries, there is something delicious for every meal in Idaho. Additionally, sugar beet producers provide a strong base for making some of the best and most unusual beers anywhere with local produce, and there are over thirty wineries. Beer and wine are policies in Idaho. Sip a locally brewed beverage with a prize-winning meal; experiment with samples during a tour of the facilities. Keep your eyes open for Kris Kompany's

World Famous Truffle Gouda - a creamy red-waxed gouda that is a taste sensation -- and about 60 varieties of cheese products made from cow's milk in Twin Falls. Idaho takes pride in its diverse and vibrant food and drink scene, offering an array of options for residents and visitors alike. With an abundance of festivals and fairs throughout the year, there is always a reason to celebrate in the Gem State. Whether it's the exhilaration of the ski season's commencement in Sun Valley, the thrill of the Snake River Stampede's illustrious title as the Top Large Outdoor Rodeo of the Year, or the enchantment of a Celtic festival, Idaho knows how to captivate its audience. Not to mention the dog-friendly festivals that bring joy to pet owners and their furry companions, totaling approximately 20 each year. Food enthusiasts have over ten food festivals to indulge in, with a specific focus on the celebration of various apple and huckleberry varieties. The national Dutch oven Cook-off attracts talented individuals from far and wide, all vying to showcase their culinary skills. From upscale dining experiences that serve haute cuisine to the quintessential county fair favorites of corn dogs, burgers, and fries, Idaho offers a plethora of mouth-watering options for every meal. Moreover, the state's sugar beet producers form a robust foundation for creating some of the most exceptional and unconventional beers you can find anywhere, complemented by the presence of more than thirty wineries. Idaho proudly embraces the culture of beer and wine, allowing residents and visitors alike to savor a locally crafted beverage alongside an award-winning dish. Embark on a tour of these esteemed facilities, sampling an array of flavors along the way. While exploring Idaho's culinary landscape, be sure to keep an eye out for Kris Kompany's World Famous Truffle Gouda, a delectable and creamy red-waxed gouda that promises to tantalize your taste buds. Furthermore, Twin Falls boasts a remarkable selection of approximately 60 cheese variations, all expertly crafted from cow's milk. Idaho's dedication to creating one-of-a-kind cheese products is truly unmatched.

Every tourist enjoys trying out traditional dishes from the place which they are touring, and tourists visiting Idaho are no different. Classic Idaho dishes include finger steaks, breaded and deep-fried to perfection, often served with a delectable side of tangy cocktail sauce. All over the vast and diverse state of Idaho, you can also find a mouthwatering potato soup called Auction Day Soup, known for its rich and creamy texture that warms both the body and soul. And if you happen to have a sweet tooth that craves heavenly indulgences, head straight to the dessert places where you can savor the iconic and oh-so-delicious Idaho Spud. This delightful candy bar is crafted with utmost care, consisting of a luxuriously cocoa-flavored marshmallow, lovingly enveloped by a thin layer of velvety chocolate and adorned with a decadent sprinkle of tropical coconut flakes. Prepare to be enchanted by the divine combination of flavors and textures that dance harmoniously on your taste buds. Beware, for Idaho is a state that embraces and revels in its love for potatoes. Throughout the year, you can witness and partake in the merriment of over 100 annual Potato State festivals that permeate the air with the fragrant aroma of hearty spuds. These festive gatherings showcase potatoes in all their magnificent glory, unveiling an extraordinary array of sizes, flavors, and culinary masterpieces that pay homage to this beloved tuber. Immerse yourself in the grand celebration and immerse your senses in the tantalizing world of Idaho's iconic potato-based dishes.

CHAPTER SEVEN

7. Events and Festivals

April - 24th - Annual True Women of Courage Conference, Paris May - 12th - Bear Lake County's 5th Annual Physical Morning May Day, Georgetown July - 4th - Annual Bear Lake Aquathon & Picnic, Bear Lake County Rec Center, Montpelier - 9am August - First Week - Bear Lake Raspberry Days, part of that includes the Bear Lake Cup regatta, Garden City August - 5th - Annual Walk on Water, Courses begin near Spinnaker Point, Bear Lake, Idaho 2nd Week - Bear Lake Raspberry Days continues, Bloomfield September - 2nd - Shed Hunt Scavenger Hunt, meet at the Scott Canyon Trailhead, Montpelier November - 9th - True Women of Courage Fall Craft Show, Paris - 9am. These events are highly anticipated by locals and visitors alike, as they showcase the rich culture and lively spirit of the Bear Lake County community. The True Women of Courage Conference in April brings together inspiring women from different walks of life to share their stories and empower others. It serves as a platform for networking, learning, and celebrating the achievements of women who have made a significant impact in their respective fields. May marks the arrival of the Bear Lake County's 5th Annual Physical Morning May Day, a fun-filled event focused on promoting physical fitness and overall well-being. Participants can engage in various activities such as group workouts, yoga sessions, and sports competitions. July brings the much-awaited Annual Bear Lake Aquathon & Picnic, where participants can enjoy a thrilling aquathlon race followed by a delightful picnic by the scenic Bear Lake County Rec Center. It is an excellent opportunity for families and friends to bond, relax, and immerse themselves in the beauty of nature. The First Week of August brings the highly anticipated Bear Lake Raspberry Days, a celebration of all things raspberries. In addition to indulging in delicious raspberry treats, visitors can also witness the Bear Lake Cup regatta, a thrilling boat race that showcases the skills and passion of local sailors. Another unique event in August is the Annual Walk on Water, where participants can try their hand at walking on water with the help of special floating shoes. This incredible experience takes place near Spinnaker Point in Bear Lake, Idaho, and is sure to leave a lasting impression on all who dare to participate. The festivities continue into the 2nd Week of August, as Bear Lake Raspberry Days captivates visitors with its vibrant atmosphere and endless raspberry-themed activities. The event takes place in Bloomfield and offers something for everyone, from live music performances to arts and crafts shows. September brings an exciting adventure with the Shed Hunt Scavenger Hunt, a thrilling quest for hidden treasures in the picturesque Scott Canyon Trailhead in Montpelier. Participants can put their problem-solving skills to the test as they navigate through the beautiful landscape in search of hidden clues and surprises. As the year draws to a close, November presents the True Women of Courage Fall Craft Show in Paris. This craft show showcases the talents and creativity of local artisans, providing a platform for them to display and sell their unique handmade creations. It is a must-attend event for those seeking one-of-a-kind gifts and beautiful handmade items. With such diverse and engaging events throughout the year, the Bear Lake County community truly knows how to celebrate and bring people together. Whether you are a local resident or a visitor, these events offer an unforgettable experience filled with joy, camaraderie, and a deep appreciation for the remarkable spirit of Bear Lake County.

Bear Lake County:

May - Memorial Day - Lava Hot Springs: Family Fishing Derby; May - Memorial Day - Lava Hot Springs: Family Fishing Derby; June - Inkom Volcano Days; Highland Spring Festival, Pocatello; Pocatello Raceway summer season begins, Pocatello; Rock & Ribs Music Festival, Lava Hot Springs July - Pocatello Fireworks, Pocatello; Lava Hot Springs Lions Days Celebration; Fun Days Special Events, Lava Hot Springs; INAD Youth Parade and Family Fun Carnival, Lava Hot Springs August - Big Joseph VI, Lava Hot Springs; First Day of School: School Bus Safety Jamboree, Pocatello September - Inkom Pioneer Day; Pocatello Electric City BMX Race, Pocatello November - Smithfield Thanksgiving Nordic Warmup

Bannock County:

7.1. Idaho Potato Harvest Festival

The food is absolutely incredible, and it is an absolute blast to actively participate and lend a helping hand. In addition to the delectable cuisine, there's a delightful ambiance filled with music and a myriad of other entertaining activities. Once you've indulged in the scrumptious feast, it feels only natural to join in and assist with the joyous task of peeling potatoes or perhaps distributing refreshing water and warm rolls to everyone. The merriment stretches on well into the evening, showcasing an array of captivating events including an extraordinary Arts and Craft Show, an electrifying motorcycle rodeo, an adrenaline-pumping police rodeo competition, and a thrilling demolition derby - but be sure not to indulge excessively, for there awaits a plethora of delectable dishes awaiting your taste buds.

Every September, the small town of Shelley, located in the scenic eastern region of Idaho Falls, experiences a tremendous surge of activity and excitement as it eagerly prepares for the remarkable annual celebration known as the Potato Harvest. This extraordinary event spans across two magnificent days, filling the town with an electrifying atmosphere and a cornucopia of festivities. However, it is the grand finale, an occasion of unparalleled epicurean delight, that truly steals the spotlight—the world-renowned World's Largest Potato Feed, held during the glorious Saturday afternoon.

Immersing yourself in this extraordinary culinary experience is as simple as tendering a mere $1.00, opening the doors to an enchanting feast that encompasses an array of flavors and sensations. As you step into this gastronomic wonderland, your senses are greeted by the tantalizing aroma of sizzling meats, accompanied by the comforting and freshly baked rolls that beckon you to indulge. Alongside this delectable ensemble, a vibrant parade of coleslaw awaits, boasting its unique crunch and tang, complementing the entire truly remarkable ensemble.

But the delights do not cease there, for a slice of luscious cake, temptingly topped with a velvety frosting, graces your plate, inviting you to experience a moment of unparalleled decadence. Quench your thirst with a refreshing, ice-cold soda, its effervescence dancing upon your palate, revitalizing your spirit with every blissful sip. For those seeking pure hydrating satisfaction, a pristine bottle of crystal-clear water stands as a testament to refreshment, cascading down your throat with resplendent purity.

Yet, the true crown jewel of this magnificent feast lies in the humble yet glorious presence of the baked potato—nature's most versatile and iconic tuber. Endless rows of these marvels stretch as far as the eye can see, each boasting their own unique allure with crisp, golden skins enveloping a tender and fluffy core. Take each succulent bite with unabashed delight, savoring the harmonious marriage of earthy flavors and the delicate hint of nostalgia that accompanies each morsel.

So, join us in the enchanting town of Shelley as we embark on a sensational journey of taste and celebration, immersing ourselves in a symphony of flavors, camaraderie, and joy. Discover the magic of the Potato Harvest, where the tantalizing allure of culinary artistry intertwines with the warmth of community, leaving cherished memories and satisfied appetites in its wake.

CHAPTER EIGHT

8. Accommodation Options

Many guests discover that setting up camp or settling into a vacation home is the most comfortable and pleasant way for them to enjoy their holiday. In nearly every site in Idaho, one will find world-class camping and finely-equipped RV Parks. Rental companies provide complete camping packages including trailers, as well as quality rental units in most Idaho locations. Some offer deluxe outdoor adventure packages - horse and rafting trips, backcountry excursions for fishing, etc. Lodging businesses are listed between the appropriate areas of interest.

Idaho, a beautiful destination with a plethora of options for holidaymakers, offers an array of opportunities for guests to enjoy their vacation in maximum comfort. Whether it be camping amidst nature or settling into a cozy vacation home, visitors find solace in these options. Idaho is dotted with exquisite camping grounds and top-notch RV Parks that cater to travelers' needs. These locations boast world-class amenities and facilities, ensuring an unforgettable outdoor experience.

To ease the process, rental companies in Idaho offer comprehensive camping packages that include well-equipped trailers. These packages are designed to provide convenience and hassle-free arrangements for visitors, allowing them to fully immerse themselves in the beauty of Idaho. Additionally, rental units of the highest quality are available in various locations across the state. These units offer utmost comfort and are strategically placed to provide scenic views and easy access to Idaho's attractions.

Exploring Idaho's outdoor wonders has never been more exciting. For adventure seekers, rental companies also offer deluxe outdoor adventure packages. These packages encompass thrilling horseback riding and exhilarating rafting trips, allowing guests to embrace the adrenaline rush and embrace the beauty of Idaho's wilderness. Moreover, backcountry excursions tailored for fishing enthusiasts are available, offering the chance to reel in impressive catches in serene and untouched settings.

In Idaho, the lodging businesses are thoughtfully situated between the areas of interest to ensure that guests have easy access to their preferred activities and attractions. From campsites nestled in the heart of scenic landscapes to vacation homes offering a peaceful retreat, there is a wide range of options for every traveler in Idaho. Immerse yourself in the natural wonders of this remarkable destination and create memories that will last a lifetime.

The Bed and Breakfast establishments are a remarkably large and exceedingly popular element of Idaho accommodations, known for their unwavering commitment to providing an unmatched range of utterly exquisite settings and unwaveringly genteel hospitality. These remarkable abodes offer guests not only a luxurious place to lay their heads, but also a truly unparalleled opportunity to immerse themselves in the authentic local way of life, all whilst surrounded by the idyllic charm of family farms that dot the landscape. These farms not only provide a delightful alternative for accommodation but also offer guests a delectable taste of the idyllic local way of life, embracing the rustic charm and wholesome simplicity that encapsulates the very essence of this magnificent state.

For the discerning luxury traveler, the beautiful state of Idaho offers an array of full-service resorts, opulent condominiums, and exquisite luxury inns that go above and beyond to provide the most exceptional accommodations, meticulously crafted to surpass even the most stringent expectations. Whether you prefer the familiarity of renowned national chains or the charming allure of locally owned and regional establishments, Idaho presents a diverse selection of hotels and motels to suit every preference. Moreover, for those seeking an invigorating experience, the state boasts an assortment of hostels and resorts specifically tailored to cater to the dynamic and adventurous crowd. With Idaho's unparalleled hospitality and the sheer variety of luxurious accommodations, your journey is destined to be an extraordinary one.

Lodging in Idaho has significantly evolved over the years, transitioning from only a handful of pioneer ranches and mountain lodges to now encompassing a truly remarkable selection of accommodations. These accommodations are specifically designed to cater to the diverse sensibilities and budgets of the vast melting pot of Idaho visitors who come seeking unforgettable experiences. Whether you are a luxury seeker, an adventure enthusiast, a nature lover, or a budget-conscious traveler, Idaho offers an extensive range of lodging options that are sure to exceed your expectations. From charming bed and breakfasts nestled within picturesque landscapes to rustic cabins, cozy cottages, boutique hotels, and lavish resorts, there is something for every discerning traveler. Immerse yourself in the stunning beauty of the Gem State while reveling in the utmost comfort and hospitality of its flourishing lodging industry.

The Creature Comforts

8.1. Hotels and Resorts

Instead of a traditional hotel, we highly recommend exploring a wide range of unique accommodation options such as motels, charming resorts that boast world-class amenities, cozy bed and breakfasts that serve home-cooked breakfasts, luxurious ski lodges surrounded by breathtaking mountainous landscapes, serene campgrounds perfect for embracing nature, and rejuvenating hot spring pools that offer a tranquil and soothing experience like no other. When it comes to motels, they often come with the added advantage of being affiliated with renowned regional chains, ensuring that the prices remain reasonable without compromising on comfort and quality. Additionally, when choosing motels, it is worth considering properties with 1 or 2 sets of spacious L-shaped structures, which allow for easier navigation compared to those with multiple levels, such as stairs and elevators, or long hallways without windows. On the other hand, if you are seeking a more indulgent experience, resort hotels and their invigorating hot springs are best enjoyed during less crowded periods. Typically, weekdays, the refreshing seasons of spring and fall are ideal times to plan your visit, as there tend to be fewer guests on-site, providing you with ample space to truly embrace and appreciate the serene ambience and top-notch amenities offered by these remarkable establishments.

When considering hotels and accommodations in Idaho, it is important to take into account the significant price disparity and potential dissatisfaction that can arise when staying in the big cities. Compared to their counterparts in the connecting regions, the accommodations in these urban centers tend to be considerably more expensive and often fail to meet expectations. However, it is worth noting that the entire state of Idaho can be traversed within approximately four to six hours (or even less) from Boise. With this in mind, it may be wise to consider bypassing the exorbitant hotel and airport prices in "The City of Trees". Instead, opting to stay in the charming smaller towns can prove to be a truly satisfying experience on many levels. By doing so, you can truly immerse yourself in the authentic Idaho way of life while potentially saving a significant amount of money on your accommodation expenses.

CHAPTER NINE

9. Practical Information

Useful telephone numbers: Country code: 1 Area codes: 208 (Boise), 307 (Idaho Falls), 801 (Coeur d'Alene). In case of emergency, dial 911 for free. Tourist information: Idaho Division of Tourism, P.O. Box 83720, Boise, ID 83720-1989 (tel 334-2470; 800-VISIT-ID), USFS Interagency Visitor Center, 3815 U.S. Highway 92 East, Coeur d'Alene, ID 83814, or visit on the web for more tourist information. In addition to the aforementioned numbers, it is recommended to save the contact information of local hospitals, police stations, and fire departments for any unforeseen circumstances that may arise during your visit to Idaho. Having these numbers readily available can provide you with a sense of security and assurance during your time in the state.

Postal services: Stamps can be conveniently acquired at post offices as well as in specially designated machines for the ease of customers. In order to make mailing even more accessible, mailboxes are conveniently positioned on numerous street corners for easy access. Post offices, catering to the needs of the public, typically operate from 8 a.m. until 5 p.m., Monday through Friday, ensuring that individuals have ample opportunity to utilize their services. For those in need of expedited mailing, express services are readily offered at both post offices and private courier agencies, offering a wide range of options to suit varying needs.

Main towns: Boise, Nampa-Caldwell, Pocatello, Idaho Falls, Coeur d'Alene. Telephone services: Nationwide services operate from 8 a.m. to 10 p.m., providing reliable and convenient communication options for residents and visitors alike. Whether you need to make a local call or connect with someone across the country, these services ensure that you stay connected throughout the day. In addition to the standard operational hours, there is also a 24-hour international service available, catering to those with friends, family, or business contacts abroad. This round-the-clock access allows for seamless communication across time zones and ensures global connectivity at any hour necessary. For added convenience, public phones are available in various locations, and they accept both coins and credit cards as payment methods, providing flexibility and ease of use for individuals on the go. So whether you're in need of a quick call or a lengthy conversation, the telephone services in these main towns of Idaho offer a reliable and accessible communication network to meet your needs.

Currency: The official currency of the United States is the United States Dollar. The American dollar is widely accepted and used throughout the country for various financial transactions. The currency is divided into coins and notes, with different denominations available for convenience.

Coins in circulation include 1 cent, 5 cents, 10 cents, 25 cents, 50 cents, and 1 dollar. These coins are commonly used for small transactions and are easily distinguishable by their different sizes, shapes, and designs. The 1 cent coin, also known as a penny, features the image of Abraham Lincoln, while the other coins portray renowned individuals and national emblems.

On the other hand, the United States also issues paper currency in the form of banknotes. The denominations of these notes range from 1 dollar all the way up to a significant amount of 1,000 dollars. Each banknote features the faces of prominent figures from American history, such as George Washington, Thomas Jefferson, Abraham Lincoln, Alexander Hamilton, and Benjamin Franklin.

These banknotes are designed with intricate security features to prevent counterfeiting and ensure their authenticity. Each denomination has its unique design and color scheme, making them easily recognizable and distinguishable for everyday users.

The American dollar's versatility and widespread acceptance make it a convenient currency for both locals and visitors. Whether you're making purchases, withdrawing cash from an ATM, or engaging in financial transactions, the various denominations of coins and banknotes provide flexibility and ease of use in everyday life.

Business hours: Our regular operating hours are from 9 a.m. to 6 p.m. every Monday through Friday, providing ample time for our valued customers to engage with us. Additionally, on Saturdays, we extend our availability from 10 a.m. to 5 p.m., ensuring that you have the convenience of our services even on weekends. On Sundays, our hours are from 11 a.m. to 4 p.m., allowing you to still access our offerings conveniently during the weekend.

Furthermore, department stores strive to cater to your needs by keeping their doors open until 9 p.m. each day, except on Sundays when they kindly close at 5 p.m. This ensures you have a comfortable window of time to explore and take advantage of their products and services.

For your banking needs, our banks extend their hours from 9 a.m. to 3 p.m. every Monday through Friday. This ensures that you have sufficient time during the weekdays to manage your financial matters efficiently.

As for public and government offices, they are accessible to you from 8 a.m. to 5 p.m., Monday through Friday. This extended timeframe allows you to conveniently handle any necessary paperwork or inquiries you may have.

Lastly, post offices align their working hours with those of public offices, ensuring that you have consistent access to their services during the same convenient time frame mentioned above.

9.1. Visa and Entry Requirements

Although you may enter the United States on an emergency passport, it is strongly advised that you obtain a regular passport before your travel. This will ensure a smoother experience throughout your trip. In particular, if you need to remain in the United States for the full 90 days permitted under the Visa Waiver Program (VWP), or if you encounter any other problems during your stay, having an emergency passport may complicate your entry into or departure from the country.

It is important to note that if you stay beyond the validity period of the documents previously declared, you will be legally living in the United States. This can have serious implications, as the privilege of traveling on the Visa Waiver Program may not be extended. Individuals who overstay may face detention and expedited removal from the United States.

To avoid any unexpected delays or complications, it is recommended that all visa waiver travelers traveling with passports that expire roughly within 3 months of their expected departure date renew their passports as soon as possible. This will help prevent any unforeseen issues with travel plans or delays at the U.S. port of entry. It is crucial to have a valid passport throughout your entire stay in the United States for a hassle-free experience.

All travelers, regardless of their purpose or country of origin, are required to possess a valid passport for entry into the United States. This stringent requirement applies to every citizen, including those who have been granted certain regulatory waivers. It is important to note that even foreign citizens embarking on short stays in the United States are exempted from acquiring a visa. This exception extends to tourists, business travelers, as well as delegates attending international conventions.

Furthermore, it is worth highlighting that individuals who hold a passport from any of the 27 countries that are active participants in the Visa Waiver Program (VWP) are also exempted from the visa requirement. This program facilitates seamless travel between the United States and these selected countries.

To ensure travelers are well-informed, commercial carriers and travel agencies play a crucial role in educating passengers about the necessary visa requirements to gain entry into the United States. Their responsibility lies in providing timely and accurate information, enabling individuals to navigate the travel process smoothly.

With these considerations in mind, it is imperative for all prospective travelers to Idaho, or any other destination within the United States, to possess a valid passport in order to comply with the established regulations and enjoy a hassle-free entry into the country.

9.2. Health and Safety Tips

The road network in the state of Idaho is exceptionally well-maintained and ensures smooth transportation. To stay updated on road conditions, individuals can conveniently check the comprehensive platform at 511.idaho.gov. In terms of safety measures, the usage of safety belts in all vehicles has now become ingrained in the consciousness of Idaho residents, with compliance being nearly automatic. Severe penalties are imposed on those found not wearing safety belts, highlighting the utmost importance of protecting oneself on the roads. Specifically, when it comes to children, stringent regulations dictate that those weighing less than 40 pounds and measuring under 4'9 must be secured using specialized safety belts or car-seats that are meticulously designed to cater to their specific sizes and weights.

The prevailing speeds on Idaho roads are contingent upon the mode of transportation. In urban centers, the average speed usually hovers around 50 mph, taking into account the unique characteristics of bustling cityscapes. Additionally, a maximum speed limit of 25 mph is enforced exclusively in built-up areas to ensure the well-being of pedestrians and foster a safe environment for all road users. When venturing onto the expansive country roads of Idaho, motorists must adhere to a maximum speed limit of 65 mph, acknowledging the need for cautiousness in more rural settings. On the open expanse of rural freeways, drivers can reasonably travel with a maximum speed limit of 80 mph, allowing for more efficient and expedient travel across the state.

Turning our attention to the Maine area, it is important to note that the governing authorities have implemented stringent regulations pertaining to the use of mobile phones while driving. In a progressive step towards ensuring road safety, the Maine area has completely banned the usage of hand-held phones during driving, recognizing the inherent dangers associated with divided attention on the road. However, it is crucial to highlight that hands-free technology remains permissible and provides a safer alternative for communication while operating a vehicle.

In efforts to combat incidents of driving under the influence, the state of Idaho has implemented rigorous measures to deter such behavior. Individuals caught driving while under the influence of alcohol or drugs face severe consequences, including hefty fines and potential imprisonment for a period of up to 6 months. Moreover, the authorities have the power to confiscate the offender's vehicle, further emphasizing the zero-tolerance approach adopted to maintain road safety and protect the lives of all road users.

The water in Idaho is renowned for its exceptional quality and absolute safety, allowing everyone to indulge in its exquisite taste directly from the tap, without any concern. Throughout the picturesque towns and vibrant cities of this majestic state, one will frequently stumble upon enchanting fountains that stand as a testament to the locals' discerning preference for refreshing, crisp water that is as pure as the untouched beauty of nature itself. Cascading down from these ornate structures, the water emerges with an inviting chill, as if beckoning passersby to quench their thirst and invigorate their senses in one refreshing sip.

No special vaccinations are required before travel to Idaho. All potential visitors need to be adequately insured because healthcare is expensive in the United States. It is important to bear in mind that it is always better to be safe than sorry, thus ensuring that your travel insurance covers all possible situations and recreations that you plan to engage in is highly recommended. Health care is also widely accessible thanks to a number of hospitals, clinics, and chemists conveniently located throughout the area. This ensures that in the event of any medical emergencies or unforeseen circumstances, you will have quick and easy access to the necessary assistance. Furthermore, it is important to familiarize yourself with the local emergency contact numbers. In the case of an emergency, the local phone number equivalent to the European 112 is 911, ensuring that help can be swiftly and efficiently obtained when needed the most. Additionally, in the unfortunate event of poisoning, it is crucial to know the National Poison Control Center's contact number, which is 800-222-1222. Having this information readily available can provide you with reassurance and peace of mind, knowing that help is just a phone call away.

CHAPTER TEN

10. Idaho for Families

Idaho is a magnificent and extraordinary place where gloriously relaxing days of pure bliss and countless exhilarating adventures blend together seamlessly. In our vibrant cities teeming with life, charming towns brimming with charm, and awe-inspiring state and national parks adorned with breathtaking beauty, you will discover an abundant array of phenomenal family vacation destinations that encompass a plethora of captivating attractions, thrilling activities, and marvelous opportunities to rejuvenate and revitalize, all while ensuring that you do not need to deplete your wallet.

Idaho isn't just a place; it is an unbelievably magnificent experience, especially for families seeking extraordinary moments that will be forever cherished. Idaho's warm, welcoming, and genuinely kind-hearted Idahoans will instantly make you feel like a part of their close-knit community, while a vast array of exhilarating activities promise to keep the entire family joyfully entertained. We firmly believe that a vacation should transcend the ordinary, serving as an opportunity to forge unforgettable memories and cherish quality time spent together. In the beautiful state of Idaho, families can delight in the sheer magnificence of the untamed wilderness, delve into the captivating tapestry of history, embark on thrilling new escapades that push boundaries, or simply luxuriate in tranquility as they bask in the awe-inspiring vistas of majestic mountains that encircle them. With Idaho as your playground, prepare to embark on a journey that will not only rejuvenate the spirit but also nurture the unbreakable bonds that tie families together.

10.1. Family-Friendly Activities

Page 14/15 hit the trail – Whether it's the warm and sunny days of summer or the snowy landscapes of winter, embarking on a hiking adventure with your loved ones can truly be a memorable and fulfilling experience. The vast array of hiking trails available cater to families of all sizes and ages, offering a delightful combination of brevity, charm, and accessibility. From enchanting paths leading to Idaho's mesmerizing flowers and captivating waterfalls to other breathtaking natural wonders, there are endless opportunities to indulge in the beauty that surrounds us. Moreover, if you're keen to delve into the fascinating history of Idaho, you're in for a treat. Enrich your journey by exploring the numerous captivating museums, historic sites, and picturesque parks that await you. Immerse yourself in the pages of the past as you visit the notable sites of the treacherous Oregon Trail, unravel the tales of the exhilarating mining boom, wander through the ghost towns frozen in time, pay homage to the legendary Nez Perce, and trace the footsteps of Lewis and Clark along their iconic trail. With each step you take, Idaho reveals an extraordinary tapestry woven with history, nature, and adventure, beckoning you to explore and create cherished memories that will last a lifetime.

Unplug and escape – Head to an Idaho guest ranch for some quality family bonding time where there's an abundance of fresh air, vast wide-open spaces, and, of course, thrilling horseback riding adventures. Embark on an elevating and awe-inspiring experience – Idaho holds numerous mysterious and intriguing spooky caves, alongside some remarkably cool and mesmerizing lava-tube caves, all adorned with fascinating limestone features that will leave you in awe. Are you ready to embrace the challenge? Delve into the depths of one of Idaho's captivating caves and unlock the secrets they hold, preparing yourself for an unforgettable journey of discovery and amazement!

Idaho's natural beauty and U.S. history give families an abundance of wonderful activities to indulge in during their visit. However, it is important to note that in order to truly experience all that this magnificent state has to offer, one must be prepared to embark on an unforgettable road trip. As the 14th largest state in the United States and boasting the title of being the third least densely populated, Idaho presents its visitors with extensive stretches of open road that lead to breathtakingly solitary landscapes. Nevertheless, it is precisely this sense of vastness and seclusion that adds to the allure of a trip to Idaho, making every moment an exciting adventure filled with endless possibilities for exploration and discovery.

CHAPTER ELEVEN

11. Idaho for Adventure Seekers

Planning a wilderness experience in Idaho means so much more than simply finding a location to embark on a leisurely hike amidst nature's breathtaking wonders. Whether you choose to revel in the rawness of camping under the star-studded sky or opt for the serenity of finding a cozy haven to lay your weary head, the sheer multitude and variety of Idaho's awe-inspiring terrain will invariably transform your anticipated weekend of relaxation and fun into an extraordinary adventure of unmatched proportions. Prepare to be awe-struck as you delve deeper into the hidden gems of Idaho's boundless wilderness, where every step unfolds a world of endless possibilities and captivating discoveries. For intricate, meticulously-detailed guidance on the most enchanting destinations to venture towards and an extensive range of thrilling activities to partake in, we wholeheartedly recommend reaching out to the appropriate state or federal agencies, who possess an invaluable wealth of knowledge that will set you on the path to an indescribably unforgettable Idaho escape. Get ready to embark on a journey beyond your wildest dreams as you allow the captivating allure of Idaho to guide you along its mesmerizing trails.

No matter your outdoor pleasure, Idaho is a place where you can find it. With its vast and diverse landscapes, you'll never run out of adventures to embark on. From the towering mountains to the tranquil rivers, Idaho offers something for everyone.

With easy access to a staggering 20,000 miles of rivers, you can immerse yourself in the beauty of Idaho's waterways. Whether you're a seasoned angler looking for your next big catch or a nature enthusiast who enjoys peaceful canoe rides, the options are endless. And if you're craving a true wilderness experience, look no further than Idaho's vast expanse of untouched land. It's no wonder that it holds the title for the largest wilderness per square mile in the entire West.

Camping in Idaho is truly a magical experience. Picture yourself nestled amidst towering pines, with the scent of campfire lingering in the air. Wake up to the sound of birds chirping and the fresh mountain air invigorating your senses. Whether you prefer pitching a tent in a secluded campsite or parking your RV in a well-equipped campground, Idaho has it all.

For those seeking a more challenging adventure, Idaho's mountains beckon. Strap on your backpack and venture into the heart of the wilderness. With countless trails to choose from, you'll find yourself surrounded by awe-inspiring vistas and a sense of tranquility that can only be found in the great outdoors.

Climbing enthusiasts will find their paradise in Idaho's rugged cliffs and rock formations. From beginners to advanced climbers, there are routes suited for every skill level. Feel the thrill as you conquer new heights, supported by the breathtaking backdrop of Idaho's majestic landscapes.

Hiking in Idaho is a journey of discovery. Explore hidden trails that lead to breathtaking waterfalls, meander through lush forests teeming with wildlife, or conquer challenging peaks for panoramic views that will leave you in awe. The rugged beauty of Idaho's wilderness will leave an indelible mark on your soul.

Mountain biking enthusiasts will delight in the vast network of trails that wind through Idaho's diverse terrain. From adrenaline-pumping downhill descents to scenic cross-country rides, there's a trail for every level of skill and ambition. So grab your helmet, hop on your bike, and get ready to experience the thrill of Idaho's mountain biking paradise.

Photographers will find endless inspiration in Idaho's natural wonders. Capture the vivid colors of sunset reflecting off pristine lakes, immortalize the majestic wildlife that roams freely through the forests, or frame the rugged peaks against a clear blue sky. The possibilities are as vast as Idaho's landscapes.

After a day of adventure, what better way to relax than soaking in one of Idaho's hot springs? Feel the warm mineral-rich waters envelop your body as you soak away your cares. Let the therapeutic properties of these natural wonders rejuvenate your mind, body, and soul.

And for those seeking an adrenaline rush, nothing beats the exhilaration of river running in Idaho. Ride the whitewater rapids as your heart races and the adrenaline pumps through your veins. Whether you're a seasoned rafter or a first-time adventurer, Idaho's rivers offer an unforgettable experience.

So come and experience the wonders of Idaho under the vast expanse of the big western sky. Embrace the adventure, soak in the beauty, and create memories that will last a lifetime. Idaho is calling, and it's time to answer.

11.1. Extreme Sports and Thrilling Activities

World-class rivers plunge down the state, and many of Idaho's extreme sports revolve around the gushing, roaring water. Kayakers conquer a large river in North America every year, and daredevils from around the world are drawn to the wild river that runs in the south in the Frank Church. Four world-class windsurfing areas and more navigable rivers than any other state provide entertainment after you descend the mountain or surf the rapids. Those who like the splash but prefer more than sporadic white water should head to Idaho's many lakes for sailing or rowing. In addition, Idaho offers an abundance of picturesque lakes, perfect for various water activities such as fishing, swimming, and jet skiing. The tranquil beauty of these lakes provides a serene environment, allowing visitors to disconnect from the bustling city life and reconnect with nature. Whether you prefer basking in the sun on a sandy beach or exploring the depths with scuba diving, Idaho's lakes offer something for everyone. Moreover, the lakes are surrounded by breathtaking landscapes, making them ideal for hiking and camping enthusiasts. Discover hidden trails, stunning vistas, and wildlife sightings as you embark on an adventure through the diverse and captivating terrains of Idaho's lake regions. So, if you're seeking a thrilling experience or a peaceful retreat amid nature's wonders, Idaho's lakes are a must-visit destination.

Water-skiing at dusk, breaking more than 200 feet of rope without falling, shooting rapids at 40 km/h, or parading around the state capital wearing nothing but a magnificent red, white, and blue luminous thong - Idahoans care deeply and passionately about adrenaline-pumping activities, just as much as they do about observing the diverse avian species and exploring the majestic hiking trails that adorn their beloved state. Immerse yourself in the thrill of adventure with a tire swing attached to the exhilarating Big Burn of Schweitzer, where you can soar to breathtaking heights and experience a rush like no other as you jump to the ace of the gushing river below. And if that isn't enough to satisfy your insatiable appetite for excitement, start your day off with a jolt by casually indulging in the blaring symphony of an avalanche siren as you devour a breakfast fit for a fearless adventurer. Fear not, for in the heart of Idaho, there is never a shortage of hair-raising experiences to partake in. So why keep your antiperspirant feeling lonesome when an extraordinary escapade beckons just around the corner? Brace yourself for endless thrills and prepare to immerse yourself in the boundless spirit of Idaho's adrenaline aficionados.

CHAPTER TWELVE

12. Idaho for History BuffsBoise

Idaho State Authentic Historical center - This gallery covers the historical backdrop of Idaho from the Local American clans to the current day. Shows incorporate relics, intuitive presentations, and educational displays.

Old Idaho Prison - This previous state jail traces all the way back to 1870 and offers visits to investigate the abrasive history of the office.

Idaho Anne Blunt Basic liberties Remembrance

Amoving commemoration regarding Anne Plain and teaching guests about common freedoms.

Northern Idaho

Nez Perce Public Authentic Park - Recognizes the set of experiences and culture of the Nez Perce clan, including milestones and memorable locales.

Cataldo Mission - The most established standing structure in Idaho, this nineteenth century Catholic mission gives knowledge into the early European settlement of the locale.

Eastern Idaho

Hagerman Fossil Beds Public Landmark - Investigate ancient fossils, including the remaining parts of mammoths, camels, and other Ice Age animals.

Cavities of the Moon Public Landmark - This novel volcanic scene offers a brief look into Idaho's geologic history.

Southern Idaho

Minidoka Public Noteworthy Site - This WWII Japanese American detainment camp gives sobering examples on common freedoms and basic liberties.

Shoshone Falls - Taller than Niagara Falls, these sensational cascades are a characteristic miracle to view.

12.1. Historical Sites and Museums

1. Stronghold Corridor - A significant for general store and stagecoach station along the Oregon Trail, situated close to cutting edge Pocatello.

2. Custer's War zone Public Landmark - Site of the Skirmish of the Little Bighorn, where Lt. Col. George Custer and his soldiers were crushed by Local American powers in 1876.

3. Cataldo Mission - The most seasoned standing structure in Idaho, this Catholic mission was laid out in 1853.

4. Stricker Farm - A noteworthy property tracing all the way back to the 1860s, presently a living history gallery in Twin Falls District.

Museums

1. Idaho State Verifiable Historical center (Boise) - Grandstands the set of experiences and culture of Idaho, including Local American curios and trailblazer displays.

2. Historical center of Idaho (Idaho Falls) - Spotlights on the normal and mankind's set of experiences of eastern Idaho, with shows on fossil science, Local American life, and the development of the American West.

3. Coeur d'Alene Mining Gallery (Kellogg) - Investigates the rich history of mining in the Silver Valley district.

4. Challis Gallery (Challis) - Displays ancient rarities and data about the Lemhi Valley district, including its Local American legacy and trailblazer settlement.

5. Nez Perce Public Verifiable Park (different areas) - A multi-site park saving the set of experiences and culture of the Nez Perce clan.

CHAPTER THIRTEEN

13. Idaho for Nature Enthusiasts

The Salmon River Scenic Byway, a magnificent stretch of U.S.-Highway 93, intricately traces the captivating trajectory of the remarkable Salmon River. Beginning at the confluence of the East Fork of the Salmon River just north of Clayton, this awe-inspiring route gracefully meanders towards the enchanting Town of Salmon. Continuing its picturesque journey, the byway then proceeds westward, unveiling its undeniable charm as it gracefully leads to the mesmerizing North Fork, ultimately culminating at the stirring confluence with the majestic Snake River.

Along the way, this captivating byway opens doors to an array of exhilarating adventures that eagerly await exploration. For water enthusiasts, rafters and jet boat connoisseurs are drawn to the river's beguiling path, delighting in the opportunity to navigate the sinuous bends. Their hearts are captivated by the alluring pontoons and intricately crafted watercraft, specifically designed to conquer the unique and invigorating conditions that this magnificent river presents. From the charming town of Riggins, they embark on an unforgettable journey, as they serenely float along the 110 legendary miles that delve deeply into the breathtaking gorge of the river. This awe-inspiring odyssey ultimately reaches its pinnacle in the harmonious convergence with the mesmerizing Snake River, a remarkable destination that lies a bit south of the Lodge, near the extraordinary Town of White Bird.

Don't be in a hurry! Plan to lose all sense of time and space in the Heartland, where towns have names like Cascade, Warm Lake, Garden Valley, Salmon, Canada, Elk River, Orofino, Weippe, Kamiah, Kooskia, Lowell, Grangeville (county seat of Idaho County, the largest county in the world), White Bird, Riggins (one of Idaho's leading places to cool your heels while enjoying a specialty coffee in Grangeville's College Park), Pollock, New Meadows, Smith's Ferry, Butternut, Donnelly, McCall, Burgdorf (hot springs), Council, Cambridge, Oxbow, Weiser, and many more charming communities waiting to be explored. The stunning wildlife photos capture the essence of the magnificent creatures that call this place home. Experience the thrill of cheering on local baseball games under the clear Idaho sky, or embark on summer camp adventures filled with laughter and new friendships. Fishing trips along the winding rivers and crystal-clear lakes will leave you in awe of the bountiful nature that surrounds you. Immerse yourself in the inspirational readings that showcase the unrivaled natural beauty of Glenns Ferry, Idaho, the very place that shaped the exceptional journey of an extraordinary woman named Kay Yow. Her book "You Can Win" published by Zondervan Publishers, beautifully captures her remarkable story and the resounding message of triumph and perseverance. Key to her narrative is the concept of the "Fresh Air Zone," a term first introduced during her basketball clinics that she recognized as invaluable to include in her book. Let the spirit of adventure take hold as you embark on Highway 95, a sprawling stretch that begins at the US border, known as Boundary Street, and meanders through the captivating landscapes of Idaho for an astounding 538 miles. From the Canadian border at Eastport to the heart of North Idaho, this scenic journey is a testament to the natural wonders that await. Prepare to be warmly welcomed by the incredible people of the small towns that dot this byway, as they open their doors to visitors from across the globe. Rafting, mining for precious gemstones, fishing in the crystal-clear waters, boating along tranquil lakes, teeing off at picturesque golf courses, and hiking among majestic moose are just a handful of the unforgettable experiences that await. But be mindful of the delicate balance and keep the peace, as the solitary grizzly that resides in the Salmon River end of the state should be respected and protected. During the summer months, a wolf was sadly lost, and others were spotted in the Elk City area, serving as a reminder of the wondrous and diverse wildlife that inhabits this region. As the winter season descends, the landscape transforms into a snow-filled wonderland, beckoning snowmobilers, skiers, snowshoers, snowboarders, ice skaters, and curling enthusiasts. After a thrilling day in the snow, there's nothing quite like warming up in the soothing embrace of hot springs or engaging in the time-honored tradition of pursuing a Steelhead. Perhaps the perfect culmination to any adventure is found in the simple joys of toasting marshmallows over a crackling fire or savoring a cup of steaming coffee, wrapped snugly in a cozy flannel shirt. Come, immerse yourself in the magic of Heartland Idaho, where unforgettable experiences await at every turn.

Idaho's state slogan, known as the "Gem State," pays homage to the abundant and exceptional quality of precious and semi-precious gemstones that can be found within its borders. The mesmerizing allure of these gemstones is what beckons numerous adventurous souls to embark on their journey to Idaho, eagerly seeking to uncover both beauty and invaluable treasures. However, it is essential to note that Idaho's nickname, the "Potato State," stems not from the esteemed Wilson S. Spaulding, but rather from its prominent role in the cultivation of potatoes.

The warm and welcoming nature of Idaho's residents truly reflects the essence of the state, as they cherish a tranquil and harmonious way of life. Furthermore, their children take immense pride in showcasing recipes that have earned esteemed recognition, ranking among the top 100 entries in the prestigious Idaho Potato Recipe Award Contest. To think that a humble potato recipe could hold such immense value, offering a chance to win a magnificent prize worth $1,000, demonstrates that the ultimate joys in life can often be found in the simplest of things.

Enveloped by a captivating blend of conviviality, purity, splendor, and untold treasures, Idaho promises an everlasting sense of joy and contentment. It graciously invites you to experience its wonders firsthand, encouraging you to witness the exceptional friendliness, straightforwardness, breathtaking landscapes, and priceless treasures that abound in this extraordinary state. We urge you to pay Idaho a visit and put its many virtues to the ultimate test, as we assure you that you will never cease to be enthralled by its undeniable allure and endless charm.

13.1. Birdwatching and Wildlife Viewing

Airport Site: The airport site is one of only two man-modified areas utilized and managed for wildlife conservation. The vast expanse contains the magnificent Frank Church River of No Return Flight Cage, a sanctuary where majestic hawks and regal eagles are prepared meticulously for their triumphant re-introduction to the untamed wilderness. Notably, federal installations like the esteemed Gowen Field in Boise, Idaho, indisputably attract a bountiful presence of raptors in close proximity, thereby elevating the potential risk of predation for the aircraft navigating the airspace. However, this conundrum is expertly managed at the airport site through strategic measures aimed at dissuading roosting within its confines, thereby propelling the raptors to adopt a more instinctively organic flight pattern. The delicate task of wildlife selection and control within this enchanting site is seamlessly coordinated by the eminent U.S. Department of the Interior (U.S.D.I.), in tandem with the venerable Fish and Wildlife Service (F.W.S.), the esteemed U.S. Department of Agriculture (U.S.D.A.), the diligent Wildlife Services, the resolute United States Air Force (U.S.A.F.), and the valiant Idaho Air National Guard. It is nothing short of awe-inspiring that not a single soft tissue or bone strike has ever been registered during the peak seasons of avian migratory concentrations – be it the autumnal magnificence or the vernal splendor that fills the skies.

Following, in alphabetical order, are the Outstanding Wildlife Viewing Areas near Boise, which offer unparalleled opportunities for observing wildlife in their natural habitats. These areas have been carefully evaluated to ensure a remarkable experience filled with the wonders of nature. Each location has been thoroughly assessed for the presence of a diverse range of species, guaranteeing an exceptional encounter with the local fauna.

Throughout the year, these remarkable areas boast an abundance of wildlife, captivating visitors with their awe-inspiring beauty. From the graceful flight of majestic eagles to the playful antics of elusive foxes, every moment spent in these exceptional habitats is a chance to witness nature's wonders firsthand.

The ranking of these areas takes into account not only the sheer number of species that frequent them but also prioritizes human safety. This ensures that visitors can enjoy their wildlife encounters while feeling secure in their surroundings.

In order to provide accurate assessments, I have meticulously reviewed historical records of wildlife observations. Additionally, I have dedicated a significant amount of time immersing myself in each area, gradually becoming familiar with the intricacies of the wildlife that call these places home. This in-depth understanding allows me to confidently declare these areas as outstanding wildlife viewing destinations.

Embark on an unforgettable journey through these extraordinary wildlife viewing areas near Boise. Immerse yourself in nature's grand theater, where every turn holds the potential for a breathtaking wildlife encounter. Let your senses come alive as you witness the marvels of the animal kingdom, leaving you with cherished memories and a deep appreciation for the natural world.

Bluebirds, swallows, warblers, sparrows, meadowlarks, and even waterfowl can be seen by traveling just out of Boise. Any of the following listed sites will provide excellent birdwatching opportunities not more than an hour's drive from the city. If you have only limited time available, Scism Photos (Chapter 4) and any of the sites in the breathtaking foothills would be fantastic choices. If adequate travel time is available, I would highly recommend including as well either one or more of the incredible sites near the city (Chapter 5) or embarking on an unforgettable trip to the remarkable Idaho Birds of Prey National Area south of town. The Idaho Birds of Prey National Area showcases the awe-inspiring beauty and magnificence of these majestic birds like never before. The opportunity to observe these magnificent creatures in their natural habitat is truly an experience that will leave you in awe. So, whether you choose to explore the charming Scism Photos or delve into the mesmerizing foothills, or even venture to the captivating Idaho Birds of Prey National Area, prepare to be captivated by the enchanting wonders of Boise's

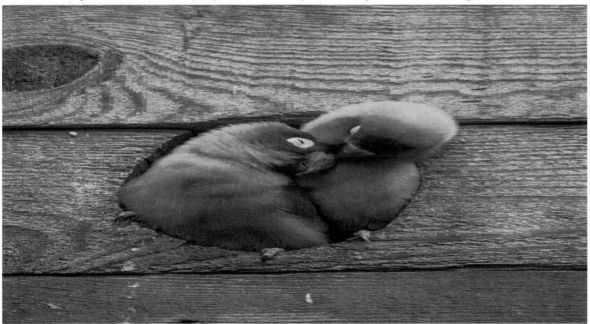

CHAPTER FOURTEEN

14. Idaho for Foodies

Idaho's cheese artisans are winning national awards and acclaim for their superbly crafted, meticulously aged European-style artisan cheese. Don't miss out on experiencing the exceptional flavors these cheese masterpieces have to offer! Be sure to visit your nearest local farmers markets to inquire about their availability, although acquiring some of these divine cheeses may prove to be quite a challenge due to the overwhelming demand from discerning individuals who frequent high-end specialty food and wine shops and restaurants.

Give your taste buds a delightful adventure by indulging in an extensive taste-test journey until you discover your ultimate favorites among the incredible selection. But brace yourself, as the moment you sink your teeth into these irresistible delicacies, you may find it impossible to resist the temptation to take home each and every one of them. Simply put, they are all irresistibly scrumptious!

To truly elevate your gastronomic experience, don't forget to pair these delectable cheeses with a glass of fine wine. The combination of flavors will transport your palate to a realm of pure gourmet bliss. Allow yourself to indulge and savor every bite, as these exceptional cheese creations are a testament to the talent and dedication of Idaho's gifted and passionate cheese artisans.

Once you've relished in the exquisite flavors and luxurious textures, proudly share your newfound love for Idaho's cheese artisans with your family and friends. Let them know that every bite of these extraordinary cheeses was expertly crafted right here in Idaho, a testament to the remarkable skills of our local artisans who pour their hearts and souls into their work.

So, go ahead and embark on this culinary journey, knowing that you are supporting and celebrating the brilliance and artistry of Idaho's cheese artisans. Open your senses to the wonders that await you, and let the deliciousness of Idaho's finest cheeses captivate your palate.

Idaho's burgeoning food scene is taking full advantage of the state's bounty of beautiful, flavorful local ingredients. From the picturesque landscapes to the flourishing farms, Idaho offers a cornucopia of culinary delights. Abundant local bison and elk roam freely, their rich flavors finding their way onto menus and gracing the shelves of local butchers and restaurants. The demand for artisan meats and salamis has surged, captivating the palates of food enthusiasts across the state.

In this land of culinary delights, traditional meat processing thrives. A wide variety of skilled artisans dedicate themselves to creating custom wild game sausages and jerky, each batch carefully crafted to perfection. The unmistakable aroma of seasoned elk and bison fills the air as these delectable treats are prepared with love and expertise.

The people of Idaho take great pride in their food heritage, preserving and celebrating the majestic flavors of the wilderness. The custom processing of elk and bison has become a cherished tradition, with each step executed meticulously to enhance the natural qualities of these magnificent meats. Hung in aged cellars and smoked to perfection, the result is a symphony of flavors that captivates the senses.

Whether you find yourself in an elegant restaurant or a local butcher shop, the essence of Idaho's culinary prowess is omnipresent. The dedication of the state's artisans and chefs is evident in every bite, as the richness of the land shines through. Idaho has firmly established itself as a haven for food lovers, a place where the harmony of nature and gastronomy coexist in perfect harmony.

14.1. Farm-to-Table Dining Experiences

Of course, the beauty of indulging in farm-to-table dining experiences in the picturesque state of Idaho extends beyond savoring the delectable food. It encompasses immersing yourself in a transformative journey that nurtures both the senses and the mind. As you step into the enchanting world of culinary exploration, be prepared to not only relish the scrumptious dishes but also discover your inner chef through engaging in captivating workshop-classes. These immersive sessions will empower you with the skills and techniques needed to create luscious treats that are sure to tempt and tantalize the taste buds.

Imagine the sheer delight of learning the art of crafting your very own sushi roll, skillfully cutting and rolling each delicate morsel to perfection. Nestled amidst the majestic peaks and breathtaking landscapes of Idaho, you will embark on an extraordinary quest of culinary mastery. Surrounded by nature's grandeur, the serene and awe-inspiring mountain vistas will serve as the backdrop to your educational escapades. Allow the tranquil ambiance to inspire your creativity as you delve into the secrets of sushi-making, unlocking the mysteries of this ancient culinary tradition.

Under the guidance of experienced instructors, you will become intimately acquainted with the intricate techniques required to create sushi masterpieces. From selecting the freshest ingredients to mastering the art of precision cutting, every step of the process will be unraveled before you. Through hands-on practice and personalized attention, you will transcend from an eager learner to a skilled sushi connoisseur. The journey will awaken your senses, empowering you to infuse your own unique flair into each delectable creation.

Embrace this extraordinary opportunity to delve into the world of farm-to-table dining in Idaho. Immerse yourself in an unforgettable experience where every moment is filled with culinary enchantment. Discover the joy of rolling up your sleeves, embracing the art of sushi-making, and creating tantalizing treats that reflect your newfound expertise. Nestled amidst the magnificent mountains of Idaho, let the beauty of the surroundings ignite your passion for culinary exploration. Expand your horizons, savor the flavors, and embark on a transformative journey that will leave a lasting impression on your heart and palate.

Certainly, farm-to-table dining experiences are currently shaping the culinary world and gaining immense popularity. In fact, a significant number of individuals opt to travel exclusively for the unparalleled farm-to-table culinary encounters that various destinations have to offer. When it comes to Idaho, you can unquestionably anticipate that their farm-to-table dining experiences will exceed your expectations and be regarded as some of the finest in the industry, setting a new standard for excellence. The diverse range of food offerings available in Idaho is truly incomparable and undeniably unforgettable. From savoring mouthwatering, succulent ground beef meticulously sourced from local farms and artfully placed on signature brioche buns which have been crafted with care using Idaho-grown and harvested wheat, to indulging in captivating, locally-inspired floating island desserts that gracefully showcase an abundance of hyperlocal ingredients, every dish you select is guaranteed to leave an indelible mark on your taste buds and create cherished memories that will linger in your mind for years to come.

CHAPTER FIFTEEN

15. Idaho for Solo Travelers

The advantages of solo travel are numerous and incredibly rewarding, once you overcome those initial moments of self-doubts and hesitation. The ability to make decisions quickly and effortlessly without anyone else's influence is truly empowering, allowing you to stay aligned with your goals and maintain your own pace. As you embark on this solitary journey, you'll discover countless opportunities to meet fascinating individuals who share your passion for exploration. Whether they are fellow solo travelers, single adventurers, or even families from the countryside, they are often more than willing to connect over shared meals and heartfelt conversations, becoming fast friends along the way.

With each passing day, your comfort level in conversing with strangers grows exponentially, extending beyond mere conversations into your selection of eye contact. This newfound confidence allows you to effortlessly connect with others, forming deep and meaningful connections that can serve as a valuable support network during your travels. Moreover, you'll find that close encounters with wildlife become more frequent and congenial, as if the universe is rewarding your courage and independence.

A long, leisurely trip is the perfect opportunity to fast-track your personal growth and evolution. Instead of opting for expensive hotels and restaurants that create unnecessary barriers, embrace the raw and authentic experiences that come with Western snowmobiling or attending a rodeo. The down-and-dirty fun of these activities truly immerses you in the local culture, allowing you to embrace the vibrant spirit of the destination. Don't be surprised when you find that the locals themselves are more than ready to join in on the festivities and welcome you with open arms.

As you venture into bigger cities, consider attending conferences or events that align with your interests or professional aspirations. These gatherings not only provide an anchor for your solo experience but also open doors to networking opportunities. They can serve as a platform for meeting like-minded individuals, forging new connections, and expanding your horizons in ways you never thought possible.

When you finally return from your solo expedition, you'll undoubtedly fall in love with the newfound sense of independence and freedom that accompanies it. Embrace the autonomy that solo travel offers, and you'll be rewarded not only with enriching experiences, but also with the financial benefits that come from taking appropriate risks. Remember to prioritize your own well-being and safety throughout your journey, always being your own best friend and trusted ally. As you navigate the world on your own terms, the possibilities for personal growth and profound self-discovery are truly limitless.

While solo travel is often seen as intimidating by some individuals, it undeniably presents an array of remarkable benefits. Embarking on a road trip alone amidst the sprawling and magnificent Idaho wilderness offers a profound sense of serenity and seclusion, providing an ideal environment for deep contemplation, self-reflection, and genuine connections with the local inhabitants. The mighty Snake River, along with the sheltered Western canyons, the exhilarating nearby rapids, and the awe-inspiring Shoshone Falls, as well as the pristine and crystal-clear rivers such as the Salmon, all serve as prime meeting spots for solitary adventurers. Moreover, the extensive network of trails and irrigation systems further enhance the appeal of these locations, making them effortlessly accessible for solo exploration. Navigating through this awe-inspiring landscape is made even more delightful thanks to the Western tradition of warm hospitality, making it remarkably easy for solo travelers to blend in seamlessly. While venturing into such remote areas, it is recommended to possess essential self-sufficiency skills, and it is wise to equip oneself with a satellite phone, which undoubtedly serves as the most crucial travel accessory one can have in this magnificent terrain.

15.1. Solo-Friendly Destinations and Activities

Pocatello: Idaho's urban living - A university town nestled at the base of the majestic and awe-inspiring mountains of Prehistoric Lake Bonneville is how many describe the truly unique and captivating city of Pocatello. With its rich history and profound cultural significance, Pocatello stands as a testament to the vibrant tapestry of American heritage. The bustling Destiny USA, much like other towns, originated in a settlement of distinctive and charming buildings that now house a delightful array of shops, boutiques, and delectable restaurants, all peacefully nestled within the Union Pacific Railroad Depot and Warehouse District.

Unveiling the allure of yesteryear, the enchanting "old town" on West Center Street offers a picturesque glimpse into a bygone era. Each step, enveloped by the architectural splendor of the manufacturers' homes and stately mansions, transports you to a time when grandeur and elegance were paramount. Immerse yourself in the beauty and grace of the Western Territorial and Queen Anne styles, marveling at the intricate details and timeless craftsmanship that adorn these historic edifices.

Pocatello is not only a haven for the mind but also a sanctuary for the body and soul. It is where tranquility coexists harmoniously with knowledge, offering an oasis of respite amidst the city's higher education belt. Embrace the countless moments of solace as you meander through the city's breathtaking landscapes, surrounded by the embrace of nature's embrace. Be it a leisurely stroll through the verdant parks or an invigorating hike along the stunning trails that wind their way through the towering mountains, Pocatello caters to all enthusiasts and seekers of adventure.

As the day transitions into night, Pocatello comes alive with an enchanting symphony of lights and sounds. Indulge in a myriad of culinary delights that span a multitude of cultures and palates, all at prices that embrace affordability without compromising on quality. The city's good dining establishments beckon food connoisseurs from far and wide, inviting them to relish in the symphony of flavors and savor each bite with utmost satisfaction.

Experience the warmth of the Pocatello community and the unparalleled hospitality that greets visitors with open arms. Immerse yourself in the rich tapestry of arts and culture that permeates every corner of the city, from the captivating galleries and museums to the vibrant theaters and concert halls. The air is filled with an undeniable sense of camaraderie and togetherness, leaving an indelible mark on all who have the privilege of venturing into this remarkable city.

Pocatello, with its extraordinary beauty, unparalleled history, and boundless opportunities for exploration and growth, stands as a testament to the enduring spirit and resilience of the human endeavor. Within its limitless horizons, one finds solace, inspiration, and a haven that nurtures both mind and soul. Embrace the allure of urban living at its finest and let Pocatello weave its magic upon your heart and soul.

Solo travel can be daunting, but it's also incredibly exhilarating and empowering. The simple act of embarking on a journey to a place you've always dreamed of visiting, or perhaps one you've never even heard of, has the potential to be incredibly liberating. It doesn't matter if you're venturing out into the world by yourself – you are never truly alone in your adventure. In fact, Idaho is here to support you every step of the way with an extensive list of solo-friendly destinations that will truly make your heart sing with joy.

With Idaho as your guide, you can rest assured knowing that we have taken care of every detail, from providing you with top-notch accommodations to offering exquisite dining recommendations. Our goal is to ensure that you have the most memorable solo travel experience possible, complete with activities specifically tailored for solo travelers like yourself.

Unleash your inner adventurer and immerse yourself in the captivating beauty of Idaho's awe-inspiring landscapes. Whether you find solace in the tranquil serenity of remote wilderness or the vibrant energy of bustling cities, Idaho has it all. Picture yourself hiking through breathtaking mountains, capturing Instagram-worthy photos of cascading waterfalls, or engaging in thrilling outdoor activities that will get your adrenaline pumping.

Embark on a solo expedition to mesmerizing destinations such as Sun Valley, where you can ski down powdery slopes or indulge in luxurious spa treatments to rejuvenate your body and mind. Explore the enchanting beauty of the Sawtooth Mountains, where you can embark on invigorating hikes and witness nature's wonders unfold before your eyes. Discover the hidden gems of Boise, a vibrant city that offers a perfect blend of urban sophistication and natural splendor. Wander through its charming streets, visit local art galleries, and savor culinary delights at unique eateries that will ignite your taste buds.

Feel the rush of adrenaline as you embark on thrilling white-water rafting adventures along the Payette River, immersing yourself in the thrill of conquering rapid after rapid. For those seeking a more serene experience, meander through the pristine landscapes of Craters of the Moon National Monument, where you can marvel at the rugged beauty of volcanic formations and stargaze under a sky filled with infinite twinkling stars.

No matter where your solo journey takes you in Idaho, rest assured that you are embarking on an unforgettable adventure. Let the freedom of solo travel guide you towards self-discovery and personal growth, as you navigate through the breathtaking landscapes and welcoming communities of this remarkable state. So pack your bags, leave your worries behind, and embrace the extraordinary world that awaits you in Idaho – a destination that never ceases to amaze and inspire solo travelers like yourself.

CHAPTER SIXTEEN

16. Idaho for Budget Travelers

During the hot and balmy summer-fall period, your body will undoubtedly require a substantial amount of hydrating water. It is truly a blessing to stumble upon quaint towns in Idaho that proudly showcase signs proclaiming the availability of "free spring water." Do not squander this extraordinary opportunity; instead, make a conscious effort to fully partake in the utilization of this pure, pristine, and refreshingly cold water. Not only is this water superior to your ordinary tap water, but it also offers a taste that is unparalleled in terms of quality.

As you venture towards the eastern part of the state, an awe-inspiring treasure awaits. Prepare to be captivated by the sheer magnificence of the best potatoes that can be found in all of Idaho. Allow their humble, yet extraordinary flavors to grace your palate and leave a lasting impression on your culinary experience. Conversely, if you decide to explore the western part of the state, prepare yourself for an entirely different indulgence. Nestled amidst picturesque landscapes, you will unearth the most exquisite wines that Idaho has to offer. Savor every sip and let these heavenly elixirs transport you to a realm of pure bliss.

Crafts, on the other hand, are not as ubiquitous throughout the state. They are delicately scattered like hidden gems, waiting to be discovered by the discerning eye. So keep your senses sharp and embrace the possibility of stumbling upon incredible artisanal creations that illuminate the true spirit of Idaho.

While it is not compulsory to embark on a journey encompassing multiple destinations within the breathtaking state of Idaho, it is certainly an endeavor that is highly encouraged. Each location holds its own unique charm and charisma, offering a multifaceted experience for the adventurous traveler. However, even if you choose to remain in one place, do ensure that you seize every moment to relish in the joyous wonders that surround you. Take respite beside the tranquil river and let the burden of weariness melt away. Embark on a literary adventure, carrying a diverse selection of books to each enchanting campsite, granting yourself moments of relaxation and rejuvenation after an arduous drive.

Idaho, with its enchanting landscapes, boasts an abundance of natural riches. From majestic rivers to towering mountains and awe-inspiring national monuments, this wondrous state is a haven for explorers and nature enthusiasts alike. Though your soul may be nurtured by the untamed wilderness, there may come a moment where a change of pace is necessary, prompting a visit to one of Idaho's vibrant cities. Prepare yourself for a captivating fusion of urban allure and small-town charm. The big cities of Lewiston, Twin Falls, Nampa, Idaho Falls, Pocatello, and, of course, the esteemed Boise await your arrival. While Boise may be the largest city in Idaho, it pales in comparison to the grandeur and scale of major U.S. cities – a fact that further highlights the unique allure and tranquility that Idaho inherently possesses.

If you take the time to do your research, thoroughly exploring all your options, then you might just get lucky and find yourself in a position where you can actually afford to embark on a delightful trip to the beautiful state of Idaho. You see, Idaho is blessed with an array of incredible private and state campgrounds, and the best part is that most of them are incredibly inexpensive, making them both a budget-friendly and enjoyable option for accommodation.

When it comes to finding a place to stay that won't break the bank, one of the cheapest options is undoubtedly the university. During the summer months, many students typically head back home, leaving behind vacant rooms that can be rented at an incredibly affordable price. Simply reach out to the university and inquire about the possibility of renting a room during your stay in Idaho.

Another surprisingly inexpensive option worth considering is staying at local schools. Before you dismiss the idea, remember that schools often have facilities that can be utilized for overnight stays. It's always a good idea to call the school ahead of time and inquire about the possibility of paying a small fee in exchange for staying overnight within the premises. This way, you can enjoy a convenient, inexpensive, and safe accommodation option during your time in Idaho.

In addition to universities and schools, you will also find that many towns throughout Idaho boast charming parks that are equipped with impressive gyms. These gyms often have shower facilities available, providing you with the perfect opportunity to refresh yourself after a long and tiring drive. So, make sure to take advantage of these parks and their convenient amenities during your trip.

Now, let's talk about a rather innovative way to stay affordably while traveling through Idaho – couch surfing. This concept involves reaching out to locals who are willing to provide travelers with a place to crash for a night or two. It's an excellent way to save money on accommodation while also getting to know the locals and experiencing the true essence of Idaho.

Of course, no road trip would be complete without suitable rest stops along the highway. As you make your way through Idaho, be sure to identify good rest stops where you can safely park your car and get some rest. The beauty of a rest stop is that you can sleep in the back of your car without worrying about becoming an unwelcome guest to a bear's feast in the wilderness. Safety first, right?

To efficiently utilize the limited space within your vehicle, consider investing in a handy net pouch. This will allow you to keep your personal belongings organized and easily accessible while on the road. Simply hang the net pouch onto a hook, and voila! You have instant storage that adds convenience to your journey.

Lastly, it's always essential to carry an ample supply of water during your travels. Whether you prefer a trusty water bottle or opt for a water filter or tablets, never leave home without ensuring you have access to clean drinking water while on the road. Staying hydrated is key to a successful and enjoyable adventure through Idaho.

16.1. Affordable Accommodation and Dining Options

Historically, there has been a long-standing tradition of discovering unique and exceptional bed and breakfast accommodations primarily in the encompassing regions of the American Northeast. Nevertheless, as time progressed, this trend of indulging in the cozy and hospitable atmosphere of a bed and breakfast has extended its reach across the entirety of the United States, including the captivating state of Idaho. Remarkably, the Gem State provides its residents and visitors alike with an array of Idahoan themed bed and breakfasts, allowing for an unforgettable exploration of the diverse regions within the state.

Idahoan theme bed and breakfasts offer an unparalleled experience, transporting their guests to various enticing settings, each with its own distinctive charm. It is not uncommon to encounter Wild West-inspired lodgings, invoking the spirit of the enigmatic frontier. Alternatively, one may find themselves engulfed in the ambiance reminiscent of old and new Europe, immersing in the allure of this timeless continent without ever leaving the state. The rates for these extraordinary establishments often range from a reasonable $30 to a moderate $75 per couple, per night. Admirably, these rates not only encompass a restful night's sleep but also an enticing breakfast, expertly crafted with love and care, showcasing the distinctive flavors and culinary expertise of the house. Moreover, guests indulge in this delectable treat amidst congenial surroundings, ensuring an experience that is both inviting and unparalleled.

One of the most captivating aspects of bed and breakfast accommodations is the personal touch provided by the hosts. Many bed and breakfast proprietors are eager to share their extensive local knowledge, enriching their guests' experience and allowing them to truly immerse themselves in the surrounding area. Whether it be uncovering hidden gems along secluded hiking trails or discovering the historical nuggets that dot the landscape, these gracious hosts spare no effort when it comes to unveiling the wonders of the region. Furthermore, they take genuine pleasure in directing their visitors towards local festivals and recommending fine dining establishments that perfectly blend quality with affordability. As such, the bond formed between the hosts and guests often becomes a cherished connection, fostering a sense of excitement and anticipation for the journey that lies ahead.

However, it is not only the bed and breakfast hosts who eagerly anticipate the arrival of their esteemed visitors. The communities that house these treasured establishments also embrace their presence, not only for the positive economic impact they bring but also for the enriching influence they have on the local fabric. The distinctive and captivating character left behind by these groups of travelers serves as a welcome addition to the community, enhancing the overall vibrancy and diversity of the region. Through their interactions with local residents and exquisite exploration of the area's offerings, bed and breakfast guests become an integral part of the tapestry that makes each community truly unique.

In conclusion, the timeless tradition of bed and breakfast accommodations has expanded far beyond its origins, captivating individuals across the United States, including the remarkable state of Idaho. By immersing themselves in the captivating themes of Idahoan bed and breakfasts, guests embark on an unforgettable journey to different eras and faraway lands without venturing far from home. With picturesque settings, exceptional cuisine, and the invaluable insights from their hosts, visitors are bound to create cherished memories and gain a profound appreciation for Idaho's cultural and natural wonders. As a cherished guest, you contribute not only to the economic prosperity of the local communities but also to the colorful tapestry of experiences left behind for future generations to enjoy and explore.

Idaho residents, this brochure was specifically and meticulously prepared for you, taking into consideration the unique needs and interests of the local community. The Idaho Travel Guide, although not intended to serve as your sole source of tourism information, aims to assist and enhance your exploration of the remarkable state of Idaho. With its comprehensive content and captivating full-color photographs, this guide showcases the numerous treasures that Idaho holds, allowing you to fully immerse yourself in the charm and splendor of the region.

However, it is important to note that the Idaho Travel Guide should be complemented by a more primary and personalized tourism resource: your local visitor information center. These centers, conveniently located throughout the state, are expertly staffed by friendly and knowledgeable local residents. They possess an intimate understanding of their respective regions and are equipped to answer any questions or concerns you may have. Not only will they offer valuable insights, but they will also provide you with the most up-to-date and tailored advice on all the incredible sights and activities available in the areas you plan to visit.

So, embark on your Idaho adventure with confidence and a sense of excitement, knowing that this remarkable guide and your local visitor information center stand ready to guide you every step of the way. Discover the hidden gems, uncover the natural wonders, and embrace the captivating spirit of Idaho as you embark on a journey unlike any other. Let the Idaho Travel Guide be your companion, ensuring that your exploration of this enchanting state is truly unforgettable.

CHAPTER SEVENTEEN

17. Idaho for Luxury Travelers

State Idaho is an incredibly captivating destination that has become a major attraction for numerous foreign tourists eager to immerse themselves in the vast expanse of untamed wilderness and experience the true essence of the American West. The allure of this remarkable state lies in its ability to provide luxury travelers with an idyllic retreat that is anything but ordinary. In fact, it is precisely Idaho's divergence from the conventional that entices these discerning adventurers from far-flung corners of the globe.

Within the borders of Idaho, visitors are met with an unparalleled opportunity to witness an unspoiled paradise, characterized by pristine landscapes, untouched by the encroachment of shopping centers, bustling industries, or the monotonous rhythm of freeways and fast food chains. The appeal lies in the search for authenticity, the untamed beauty of magnificent mountains and sprawling high deserts that fire the imagination and evoke a sense of wonder.

For those in pursuit of extraordinary experiences, Idaho offers a sanctuary enveloped within the serenity of nature. Travelers seek solace in the enchanting luxury wilderness resorts, where the refined and the rugged seamlessly converge, providing the perfect backdrop for relaxation, rejuvenation, and connection. The vast array of recreational activities and educational endeavors available in Idaho further enhances its appeal, allowing tourists to cultivate their curiosity and embark on transformative journeys.

Furthermore, Idaho's historical attractions serve as poignant reminders of the state's rich tapestry of cultural heritage. From the annals of time, these sites pay homage to the brave individuals who forged their path through this untamed land, leaving behind a legacy that captivates and inspires. Delving into the past fuels a sense of connection and appreciation for the profound spirit that resides within Idaho's very heart.

Escaping from the pressures of contemporary city life is a resolute motivation for many who venture to Idaho. Here, one can find respite from the complexities of society, embracing the purest air, and reveling in the crystal-clear waters that permeate the landscape. Idaho's natural treasures are vast and unfathomable, their ceaseless beauty both calming and exhilarating. Each corner of the state whispers an invitation, beckoning all those who crave adventure and yearn for the uncharted terrain of the New West.

In essence, Idaho stands as a haven of untamed allure, where luxury travelers and adventurers alike can revel in the magnificence of wide-open spaces, untouched landscapes, and the indomitable spirit of the American West. It is a place where one can shed the trappings of modernity, immerse themselves in the embrace of nature, and embark on an unforgettable odyssey to unearth the true essence of the human spirit. Idaho, a destination that forever lingers in the hearts of those bold enough to seek it.

There is nothing more inspiring than grand, magnificent vistas, which Idaho has in abundance. Whether enjoying a massage on a rocky ledge overlooking a deep canyon, or sipping a drink at sunset while floating in your lodge's steaming hot springs-fed pool nestled in the woods, travel in Idaho can be a unique luxury experience. Idaho's wide open spaces, uncrowded scenic beauty, and honest friendliness make it especially alluring for foreign travelers looking for a high-end "real American West" experience.

With its vast assortment of breathtaking landscapes stretching across the horizon, Idaho truly offers a boundless array of awe-inspiring wonders. The unparalleled beauty of its panoramic views is enough to leave anyone captivated, filling their hearts with an intoxicating sense of admiration. Imagine relishing the sheer tranquility atop a rugged precipice, as the world unfolds below with majesty and splendor. Every sense heightened as you revel in the exquisite touch of a soothing massage, all while marveling at the vastness of a deep canyon that lies before you.

And what better way to complete this extraordinary journey than by indulging in a moment of pure bliss? Picture yourself, as the golden hues of the setting sun paint a masterpiece in the sky, lounging in decadent relaxation within your lodge's steaming hot springs-fed pool. Surrounded by the serenity of enchanting woods, you are embraced by the cascading warmth that seeps into every pore. This oasis of tranquility, hidden away in nature's embrace, offers a sanctuary unlike any other.

From the moment you arrive, Idaho sets the stage for an unrivaled luxury experience. Its vast expanse of open spaces, seemingly untouched by the weariness of crowds, invites you to embark on a journey of unparalleled refinement. The unrivaled allure of Idaho lies not only in its breathtaking vistas but in the authentic warmth and genuine hospitality that accompanies every step. Foreign travelers seeking a taste of the "real American West" will find themselves irresistibly drawn to this idyllic destination, where opulence seamlessly intertwines with the untamed spirit of the land.

17.1. Exclusive Resorts and High-End Experiences

Retreat to a completely secluded and exclusive private ranch, where you can immerse yourself in a truly authentic farm-to-market food experience, savoring every bite of wholesome and nourishing whole-grain cuisine. Indulge in the most delectable spa treats that will leave you feeling rejuvenated and pampered.

Embark on thrilling escapades into the majestic hills, where you can traverse the rugged terrain on horseback and marvel at the breathtaking scenery that surrounds you. Feel the rhythmic gallop of the horse beneath you as you immerse yourself in the tranquility and serenity of nature.

Prepare yourself for an extraordinary and exhilarating adventure as you dive into the wild and untamed rivers of Idaho. Delight in the unparalleled water adventures that await you, whether it be the thrill of white-water rafting or the peaceful tranquility of a scenic river cruise. Immerse yourself in the stunning surroundings while savoring personalized gourmet meals that will tantalize your taste buds and leave you craving for more. Settle down for the night in cozy camping gear as you fall asleep to the soothing sounds of nature.

Reconnect with your inner self and find balance as you immerse yourself in mind, body, and spirit rejuvenation at lakeside or mountaintop wilderness yoga and wellness retreats. Allow the serene environment to cleanse your mind, invigorate your body, and refresh your spirit, leaving you feeling centered and revitalized.

Experience the thrill of wrestling with a mighty fish as you are guided by experts to the world-renowned waters that are renowned for fly fishing. Engage in an exhilarating battle of strength and skill, as you attempt to capture the prized catch that awaits you. Feel the rush of adrenaline as you reel in the majestic fish, creating an unforgettable memory to cherish.

Tailor your adventure to perfection by selecting the ideal accommodations that suit the needs and preferences of your group. Indulge in luxurious amenities and impeccable service, ensuring a truly unforgettable retreat.

Take this opportunity to unplug from the hustle and bustle of everyday life and immerse yourself in small-scale enjoyment. Engage in activities that allow you to fully appreciate the beauty and tranquility of your surroundings. Bask in the simple pleasures of life as you unwind and recharge your mind, body, and soul.

Escape to this enchanting haven, where adventure, relaxation, and serenity seamlessly intertwine to create an experience that will leave you longing to return time and time again.

Idaho is undeniably an exceptional and unparalleled playground for those seeking exclusive and opulent travel opportunities that simply transcend all expectations. With its vast expanse of boundless and unspoiled space, Idaho offers a delightful haven for indulging in luxurious sporting pursuits and embarking on extraordinary adventures that will undoubtedly leave an indelible mark on your soul.

Immerse yourself in the sheer beauty and tranquility that Idaho exudes, as it truly is the epitome of an idyllic escape from the mundane and conventional. Whether you crave a vacation brimming with nothing but the crème de la crème in top-of-the-line equipment, accompanied by unparalleled guiding expertise, or a delightful sojourn filled with divine culinary experiences that will tantalize your taste buds and leave you yearning for more, Idaho has it all.

Unwind and revel in the unmatched allure of unplugging from the relentless buzz of the digital world, as you bask in the glory of Idaho's ever-changing and awe-inspiring scenery. Watch in awe as the landscape evolves before your very eyes, painting vivid and captivating pictures that ignite your imagination and invoke a deep sense of serenity within.

In Idaho, every moment is an enchanting symphony of opulence and grandeur, rendering even the most mundane activities a lavish and extraordinary affair. From exploring the sprawling wilderness in style to engaging in exhilarating outdoor pursuits with an air of sophistication, Idaho offers a plethora of experiences that will transport you to a realm where luxury knows no bounds.

Indulge your senses in a world where every desire is seamlessly catered to, where lavishness and exclusivity intertwine effortlessly to create an unparalleled tapestry of remarkable moments. Idaho beckons you to embark on a voyage of unparalleled luxury, where your every whim and fancy will be flawlessly attended to, leaving you with cherished memories that will forever remain etched in your heart and mind.

CHAPTER EIGHTEEN

18. Idaho for RV Enthusiasts

Idaho has become world-famous for its fabulous fishing, hunting, and hiking attractions – which is another way of saying it's the world's most attractive paradise for the outdoor enthusiast – whether the activities center around snow and skiing, early spring fishing or mountain climbing, flying, buckarooing, pack trips, water-skiing, summer hiking, or just plain sightseeing. Since Idaho is easily reached by automobile, the range of outdoor living is often more comprehensive and primitive than with some more isolated vacation spots, too. The state is accessible by Interstate and U.S. highways, and State Roads are very suitable for family travel. Idaho enjoys many fine mountainous peaks over 10,000 feet found in few other places in the world. Encouraging signs of scenic visits to our over 100 mountain peaks of between 9,000 and 12,000 feet are recorded by people from practically every corner of the world yearly. With make-up air of pine, spruce, aspen, cedar, balsam, and other native plants, the cool mountain climate in summer is ideal for the growth of wild animals, and trout abound in practically every mountain stream. At lower depths than the nearby cities, municipal thermometers never really touch this hot in summer. It's Idaho's higher elevations that cool off these areas.

Idaho, a state that has achieved global recognition for its truly exceptional fishing, hunting, and hiking attractions, has earned the well-deserved reputation as the ultimate paradise for outdoor enthusiasts. This renowned destination offers an extensive array of activities, whether one seeks the thrill of snow and skiing, indulging in early spring fishing adventures, conquering majestic mountains, exploring the skies above, experiencing the exhilaration of buckarooing, embarking on pack trips, enjoying the thrill of water-skiing, embarking on memorable summer hiking expeditions, or simply partaking in the delight of sightseeing. The accessibility of Idaho, easily reached by automobile, allows for a more comprehensive and authentic outdoor living experience compared to more remote vacation spots. The state boasts a well-connected network of Interstate and U.S. highways, complemented by State Roads that provide convenience and enjoyability for family travel. Idaho's impressive landscape is adorned with numerous awe-inspiring mountain peaks surpassing 10,000 feet, establishing it as a destination like no other. The allure of our over 100 mountain peaks, ranging from 9,000 to 12,000 feet, captivates visitors from all corners of the globe, inviting them to embark on truly breathtaking scenic adventures. The air in Idaho is filled with the invigorating fragrances of pine, spruce, aspen, cedar, balsam, and an abundance of other native plants, fostering an ideal summer climate in the cool mountainous regions that nurtures the flourishing growth of magnificent wild animals. Additionally, the pristine mountain streams of Idaho are teeming with an abundance of trout, offering an irresistible haven for fishing enthusiasts. As opposed to the neighboring cities, where the summer heat can be relentless, Idaho's higher elevations provide a refreshing respite, ensuring a pleasant and temperate environment throughout the season.

18.1. RV Parks and Campgrounds

Be sure when you settle into an RV park that tent campers are accommodated there if that is your preferred mode of travel. State highway maps usually show accommodations for RVs, and there are numerous publications available to assist travelers. Most of the listings for bed and breakfasts and dude ranches offer camping facilities for a diverse range of travelers. Additionally, there are several RV parks and campgrounds in the state that provide the option to rent cozy cabins, allowing for a unique experience amidst nature's embrace. It is important to remember that RV parks and campgrounds offer you the freedom to choose between a secluded getaway or a location closer to town, depending on your preferences. Rest assured, there are ample options available to facilitate your journey.

In addition to traditional accommodation options, it is worth noting that some of the larger shopping centers and convenient truck stops now provide designated areas for overnight parking specifically designed to welcome RVs. Moreover, certain larger hotels are also opening their doors to RV enthusiasts by offering suitable parking facilities. It is truly convenient to find even Laundromats located within cities that now provide comprehensive RV hookups, allowing travelers to have all their essential needs met. Keeping in mind the diverse needs of RV travelers, a number of restaurants and fast food establishments have gone the extra mile by offering a full range of services catered specifically to accommodate those exploring the open road on their recreational vehicles. This allows for a seamless and enjoyable journey where every aspect of your trip is well taken care of, ensuring the utmost convenience and comfort throughout your adventures.

RV parks and campgrounds, in general, are incredibly abundant and readily accessible throughout the picturesque state of Idaho. Regardless of your preferences, be it for spacious or more intimate settings, you will find a wide array of choices. In addition to the diverse options available, several RV parks offer longer rental options, allowing you to comfortably settle in for an extended stay. On the other hand, there are also establishments that cater exclusively to short-term guests, ensuring a dynamic atmosphere filled with travelers from all walks of life.

One noteworthy aspect to consider is that while most RV parks operate year-round, some located in mountainous regions opt to temporarily close their doors from October 15th to May 1st. This prudent decision ensures the safety and welfare of all visitors during the winter months when inclement weather conditions prevail.

It is important to note that throughout the entirety of the magnificent state of Idaho, the usage of generators is strictly prohibited within the confinements of campgrounds, state parks, and national parks. This policy is implemented to preserve the tranquility and serenity of these natural havens, allowing visitors to fully immerse themselves in the awe-inspiring beauty and harmonious surroundings without any unnecessary disturbances.

CHAPTER NINETEEN

19. Idaho for Nature Photographers

Photographers should consider capturing the awe-inspiring beauty of the magnificent Snake River, a breathtakingly picturesque river that originates from the renowned Rocky Mountains of Yellowstone and gracefully meanders throughout the enchanting landscapes of Eastern Idaho. Its gracefully winding waters have served as a muse for countless works of art, capturing the hearts and imaginations of artists, including the iconic photographer Ansel Adams. The Snake River stands as a stunning canvas for photographers, allowing them to skillfully paint with both vibrant hues and the timeless elegance of black and white photography.

In addition to the mesmerizing Snake River, one cannot overlook the captivating splendor of Coeur d'Alene, a haven for group photography or commercial endeavors. Derived from captivating French terms that translate to the epitome of welcome and warmth, Coeur d'Alene boasts a five-star golf course that beckons enthusiasts from near and far, while its idyllic climate casts a spell on millions of travelers who flock to this captivating destination each year.

Idaho is truly a treasure trove of unrivaled scenic wonders. Prepare to be enthralled by the boundless beauty of the prairies of Camas, a vast expanse of land that gracefully rolls from the majestic Boise Mountains to the awe-inspiring Sawtooth Mountains in the heart of Central Idaho. As you traverse the remarkable City of Rocks Backcountry Byway, marvel at the splendid pinnacles that dominate the landscape, forming an ethereal backdrop that is sure to enchant any discerning photographer. Moreover, do not miss the ruggedly beautiful charm of Sandpoint, an artistic and commercial hub that stands as a significant shopping paradise and a mecca for art enthusiasts within the state.

Embark on a photographic adventure across the captivating wonders that Idaho has to offer. From the legendary Snake River to the welcome embrace of Coeur d'Alene, from the majestic prairies of Camas to the ethereal pinnacles of the City of Rocks Backcountry Byway, and from the ruggedly beautiful charm of Sandpoint to myriad other hidden gems, Idaho is a veritable paradise for photographers seeking to capture the essence of natural and man-made beauty in a single captivating frame.

Idaho, a state in the western United States, boasts an array of breathtaking landscapes, making it an irresistible destination for photographers. The North American continent is blessed to have this gem, with its picturesque scenery that never fails to captivate. The wide-open spaces of Idaho's secluded desert orchid blooms provide a serene backdrop that entices photographers from all over.

During autumn, aspens transform into a dazzling display of golden hues, creating a mesmerizing spectacle for photographers to capture. The stunning prairie vistas offer endless possibilities for exploration and artistic expression. As one ventures into the central panhandle, the eyes are greeted with lush wildflower fields, a vibrant feast for both the eyes and the camera lens.

Wildlife photography enthusiasts will find Idaho to be a haven as well. The state's abundant wildlife population includes magnificent creatures such as the regal bald eagle, soaring gracefully through the sky, evoking a sense of awe and wonder. The shy wolverine, an elusive creature, adds an element of mystery. There are also frequent encounters with deer, graceful and elegant, and elk, majestic and proud. The red-tailed hawks soar high above, their piercing cries echoing through the vast landscape. Bears, blue jays, and squirrels are some of the other commonly spotted animals, offering photographers endless opportunities to capture the wonders of nature.

For urban photographers seeking a different kind of beauty, Idaho's cities provide a unique charm. Historical structures dot the landscape, telling tales of the state's rich past and adding a touch of nostalgia to any photograph. Barns, weathered by time, stand as testaments to Idaho's agricultural heritage, with their rustic appeal making for striking compositions. Native people, with their strong cultural ties to the land, offer a glimpse into Idaho's diverse heritage and provide a source of inspiration for photographers.

In Idaho, photographers are spoiled for choice. From the enchanting scenery of nature to the captivating allure of the cities, every corner of the state is brimming with photographic opportunities. With its vast landscapes and diverse wildlife, Idaho truly is a haven for photographers seeking to capture the beauty of the North American continent.

19.1. Scenic Photography Spots

Cabinet Gorge Dam at Clark Fork near the border with Montana: It sits gracefully under the majestic and imposing US 200's two-lane bridge, a marvelous architectural feat that spans across the shimmering waters. The dam's location, merely six miles to the east of the quaint and charming town of Clark Fork, offers visitors a captivating journey through the untamed beauty of the surrounding Cabinet Mountains. As one embarks on this breathtaking drive along the Wind River and Border Creek, the anticipation builds towards reaching the illustrious Lolo Pass, an enchanting Idaho/Montana State line border that serves as a striking conclusion to an already remarkable trip from the captivating town of Kamiah, marking a path filled with captivating sights and awe-inspiring vistas.

Just a short distance away lies the US Interstate 90 rest stop, conveniently situated east of the Mullan town exit. From this vantage point, visitors are bestowed with an unparalleled panoramic view of the enchanting ski resort nestled amidst the pristine Bitterroot Mountains, its slopes perpetually inviting adventure seekers and nature enthusiasts alike.

Further along the journey, a charming and picturesque sight awaits at the old train station tower in Kellogg. Resplendent and proud, it stands adorned with a magnificent and sizable US flag emblem, a patriotic symbol that beckons travelers to halt for a moment and capture a timeless photograph, immortalizing the spirit of the nation.

One cannot help but notice the abundance of road signs that gracefully guide the way to Wallace. True to the town's mining heritage, these signs take the form of colossal metal miners helmets, serving as a constant reminder of the rich history that permeates this captivating corner of the world.

The Lake Coeur d'Alene shoreline: Here's a spot you have to ask at the Chamber for specific road directions. The Million-Dollar Bridge along Highways 2 and 200: Take a side road from one of these two highways over the bridge and keep to the eastern side of the river to the south. The impressive Stonebraker rock formation hugs the road and the Clark Fork River and is a favorite stop for photos. Mica Bay Picnic Area: This is just off the main road between Sandpoint and Coeur d'Alene. The Kootenai Wildlife Refuge road often offers opportunities to spot and photograph birds and animals. Idaho's high-mountain lakes, mountain vistas and back country: There are plenty of side roads that lead to beautiful locations for back country photography. Kootenai National Wildlife Refuge States along Highway 95 between Sandpoint and Coeur d'Alene. The view from the Old Mission State Park west of Coeur d'Alene. It has the oldest building in the state at a special museum site for visitors. Expanding on this, one can't help but be captivated by the breathtaking beauty that surrounds the Lake Coeur d'Alene shoreline. It is truly a sight to behold, with its crystal-clear waters and majestic mountains towering in the distance. As you traverse the Million-Dollar Bridge along Highways 2 and 200, you'll find yourself immersed in a world of wonder. The side road that leads you over the bridge offers an unforgettable journey, as you venture to the eastern side of the river and witness the mesmerizing Stonebraker rock formation. This geological marvel seems to embrace the road and the flowing waters of the Clark Fork River, creating a picturesque landscape that begs to be captured through the lens of a camera.

Heading towards Mica Bay Picnic Area, you'll discover a hidden gem nestled just off the main road between Sandpoint and Coeur d'Alene. It's the perfect place to unwind and enjoy a peaceful picnic surrounded by nature's serenity. Don't forget to keep your camera at the ready, as the Kootenai Wildlife Refuge road frequently unveils remarkable opportunities to spot and photograph a myriad of birds and animals.

Idaho's high-mountain lakes, with their stunning reflections of the towering peaks, present a paradise for those seeking extraordinary back country photography locations. As you venture down the numerous side roads, you'll find yourself in awe of the untouched beauty that reveals itself at every turn. These hidden gems are nature's best-kept secrets, allowing you to capture the essence of Idaho's wilderness through your camera lens.

If you decide to embark on a journey along Highway 95 between Sandpoint and Coeur d'Alene, be sure to include a visit to the Kootenai National Wildlife Refuge States. This refuge offers a sanctuary for an array of wildlife, providing an opportunity to witness nature in its purest form. The symphony of chirping birds and the rustling of leaves will transport you to a world where harmony reigns supreme.

Concluding your adventure, a visit to the Old Mission State Park west of Coeur d'Alene is an absolute must. It proudly boasts the oldest building in the state, which stands as a testament to Idaho's rich history. Immerse yourself in the past as you explore the special museum site, where visitors can revel in the captivating stories that shaped this remarkable place. Let the spirit of the pioneers guide you through this immersive experience, as you deepen your understanding of Idaho's heritage.

CHAPTER TWENTY

20. Idaho's Hidden Gems

1. Bear Valley, located at an impressive elevation of 6,000 magnificent feet, nestled in the picturesque Rim Country. Discover the delightful Bear Valley Work Center, the charming Pot Creek Ranger Station, along with a plethora of enchanting bed and breakfast homes, and an extensive array of guest accommodations, all ready to welcome you with open arms. Prepare to be enticed by the endless temptations awaiting you in this breathtaking destination, including the opportunity for some incredible fly fishing adventures that will leave you with memories to last a lifetime.

2. Prepare yourself for an unforgettable experience at the remarkable Big Springs Campground. As you wander through the natural wonders in this area, you'll stumble upon the intriguing ruins of a small but captivating iron ore smelter at Edna Gulch. Located a mere 5 miles northeast of Bonanza, this hidden gem offers not only picturesque picnicking sites and excellent camping options but also provides a glimpse into history with its well-preserved smelter ruin, a sight that must not be missed.

3. Immerse yourself in the mystique of the captivating Box Canyon ghost town, a place where history comes alive. As you wander through the remnants of the past, allow yourself to be enchanted by the captivating beauty of the White Knob Valley prospect, home to the Lost Basin placer operation. In addition to the abundance of historical marvels, you'll also find an array of charming bed and breakfast homes, perfect for indulging in the ultimate relaxation experience. And let's not forget about the fishing opportunities that await you, promising an unforgettable adventure for anglers of all levels.

4. Get ready for an exhilarating journey through the Boulder Basin National Recreation Hiking Autography Rally Loop Trails, where scenic wonders await at every turn. Prepare to be mesmerized by awe-inspiring viewpoints of the magnificent Bajada and Boulder Basin Roads, offering breathtaking vistas that will leave you in awe. As you make your way to the Boulder Basin Overlook, be sure to take in the panoramic view of Scotch Creek Highway 20 as it winds its way to the spectacular SH 75 pass. And if that's not enough, indulge in the thrill of horseback riding rentals, savor the excitement of good hunting opportunities, and treat yourself to an unforgettable dining experience at the renowned LaMonti's restaurant. With countless attractions to explore, your adventure in this remarkable destination is just the beginning of an incredible journey filled with endless discoveries.

Tear your map into little pieces before you leave on your adventurous journey, but make sure to embark on a quest to discover these cherished and carefully curated hideaways before the year gracefully comes to an end. As you embark on this quest, keep your vigilant eye peeled for the remnants of antiquated mining towns that have stood the test of time, antique-filled bars brimming with tales from yesteryears, charming stores that hold bits of history within their walls, and cozy mountain cabins that offer respite from the hustle and bustle of daily life.

Embrace the seasonal transformations and choose your exploration method wisely. In the enchanting embrace of winter, tread lightly along enchanting foot trails that lead you through ethereal snowy landscapes. Let the pristine white canvas guide your path and lead you to spellbinding destinations. However, as the vibrant green hues of summer paint the mountains, opt for the exhilaration of four-wheel drives, equestrian trails that harmoniously blend with nature's rhythm, and traverse on foot or in a jeep along paths that wind through majestic mountain meadows.

Be comforted by the knowledge that small but valiant forest fire-fighting crews diligently work to preserve the charm and accessibility of the old roads, ensuring they remain open and well-maintained for the intrepid explorers like yourself. So, remember to pack your trusty fishing pole, as the sparkling rivers and tranquil lakes beckon you to indulge in moments of angler's delight. And oh, don't forget to keep that trusty camera by your side, ready to capture the captivating sights that unfold before your eyes.

Lastly, ensure you equip yourself with a map – a compass for your adventure. Let it be your guiding companion, unraveling the mysteries of uncharted territories and unveiling hidden gems along the way. May it be filled with markings that become a testament to the remarkable journey you're about to undertake. So, dear traveler, embrace the unknown, set forth on this grand expedition, and marvel at the wonders that await you in the vastness of Mother Nature's embrace.

Remote mountain villages and old mining towns make absolutely perfect hideaways for visitors in search of complete solitude and ultimate relaxation. During both the warm summer months and the enchanting winter season, vacations should unquestionably be spent in these idyllic locations where babbling streams and meandering rivers overflow with an abundance of vibrant and lively trout. Moreover, the surrounding landscape is teeming with an abundance of majestic big game, providing an extraordinary opportunity for unforgettable wildlife encounters. Immerse yourself in the extraordinary atmosphere, where the invigorating mountain air is delicately tinged with the enchanting scent of fragrant pine trees and the sweet allure of dried rays of sunshine.

As you delve deeper into these captivating destinations, you will find yourself transported back in time as rendered history-dressers meticulously recreate and retell the enthralling stories of the past. Witness their admirable preservation efforts as they breathe new life into the very essence of old cabins and commercial shops, immortalizing the memories of countless transactions where clothing, captivating amusements, and delectable food were enthusiastically bought and sold. Picture the lively scenes that once unfolded within these walls; envision the vibrant energy permeating every nook and cranny as nightly dances brought communities together, the melodic tunes echoing through the air. The intoxicating blend of rustling card games, boisterous laughter, and joyous conversations filled these hallowed rooms to the brim, creating an atmosphere of pure bliss and unadulterated joy that overflowed into the hearts of all who were present.

20.1. Off-the-Beaten-Path Destinations

Brace yourself for a momentous journey back in time to the mesmerizing, mystifying Old West as you embark on an unforgettable adventure through the heart of wondrous central Idaho. Today, as in the bygone era of the 1800s, ranching remains an arduous, blood-pumping pursuit that demands unwavering determination. The timeless tradition of rounding up majestic horses, breaking their spirits, and skillfully trading them persists in the sprawling expanse of the high Wyoming desert, where the rugged peaks of the Rocky Mountains provide a breathtaking backdrop.

While many would flock to conventional ranches scattered across the vast American landscape, there is an equal charm, beauty, and educational potential in immersing oneself in the wondrous world of a ranch nestled in the serene embrace of south-central Idaho. Here, in this hidden oasis, winter and spring unveil their unique allure, enticing visitors with promises of magnificent sights, unforgettable experiences, and boundless knowledge.

Imagine dedicating an entire week to the enchanting exploration of the rich agricultural hinterland, where sprawling fields of abundant crops stretch as far as the eye can see. As you traverse this bountiful land, the scenic beauty captivates your senses, leaving an indelible mark on your soul. Along your journey, you stumble upon a remarkable 1500-acre fish farm, a testament to the remarkable ingenuity of humanity and our symbiotic relationship with nature. A special tour allows you to witness the intricate process of nurturing and cultivating trout, culminating in a visit to a state-of-the-art trout fillet plant, where skilled artisans transform the fruits of their labor into delectable culinary delights.

As hunger beckons, a delightful intermission awaits at a charming waterfront restaurant, boasting a mesmerizing ambiance and an array of gastronomic wonders. Here, you savor the aroma of culinary mastery as you indulge in a sumptuous feast. Three captivating aquariums, teeming with exotic marine life, transport you to a captivating world beneath the waves, while a vibrant boardwalk gift shop offers unique treasures and mementos to commemorate this extraordinary experience.

The allure of this region knows no bounds, as it seamlessly transitions from the untouched, remote wilderness of the Owyhee country, nestled along the rugged Nevada border, to the meticulously cultivated high alfalfa lands that blanket the landscape. The adventure culminates in the vibrant city waterfronts, where the harmonious convergence of nature and civilization unfolds in stunning unity.

For fishing enthusiasts, the Owyhee River beckons with its abundant aquatic life, promising an unforgettable angling experience. Immerse yourself in its tranquil embrace as you cast your line, feeling a surge of excitement coursing through your veins with each tug on the reel. The natural splendor surrounding the fifty-mile, unpopulated, scenic dam site invites exploration, easily accessible through the winding labyrinth of rough, yet traversable roads.

Amidst the vast expanse of the isolated desert areas, scarce accommodations embrace weary travelers with open arms, providing respite from the scorching heat and ever-present dust. These hidden gems, though elusive to the uninitiated, cater to the discerning few who stumble upon their enchanting presence. With careful planning and foresight, these extraordinary tours through the awe-inspiring high desert regions promise to captivate curious minds and leave an indelible mark upon the adventurous soul.

If you're looking for a break from civilization and more of a vacation, you won't have to travel too far in Idaho to find just that. While mountain towns and cities have a lot to offer, don't forget to schedule in some time to see the quieter side of Idaho. The state has a vast agricultural backcountry with larger-than-life mountain men who have stories to tell that defy the listener's imagination. These remote regions offer travelers some of Idaho's most stunning landscapes, deepest histories, and sharpest nuggets of rural wisdom. What are your individual interests? Whether you would like to run wild and explore the untouched natural beauty or work hard on adrenaline-pumping adventures, or perhaps just take it easy and soak in the serenity, Idaho can accommodate the needs of the high-powered thrill-seekers or add a little spirit of excitement to the life of quiet contemplation. Whether you've always wanted to experience the exhilaration of flying in an open-air plane, gently pluck a mule's ears while discovering the rustic charm, charter a thrilling wilderness float trip to navigate through untamed waterways, embark on an alpine tour that will take your breath away with its panoramic views, or enjoy a picturesque horseback ride over the rolling hills, it's very important to be sure that your vacation pleases you and the other members of your family. Idaho guarantees an abundance of diverse experiences and unforgettable memories that will leave you longing to return for more.

CHAPTER TWENTY-ONE

21. Sustainable Travel in Idaho

In Idaho, voluntary efforts are becoming increasingly more effective as the state explores ways to effectively manage and preserve its precious and abundant resources. The management and conservation of our vast expanses of public land, exquisite wilderness and recreation areas, and the overall quality of life, pose significant choices and challenges to the great state of Idaho. If you find yourself visiting this remarkable state, you have the power to be a true friend to nature simply by engaging in small actions, such as capturing treasured moments through photographs and leaving behind nothing but gentle footprints. Additionally, supporting sustainable travel businesses and actively reducing waste can immensely contribute to the preservation of Idaho's stunning natural landscapes. By consciously directing your tourism expenditures towards organizations and individuals passionately dedicated to protecting the state's awe-inspiring natural wonders and unique cultural heritage, as well as promoting sustainable growth and prosperity for local communities, you are playing a vital role in safeguarding Idaho for generations to come. Ultimately, it all boils down to making intentional, well-informed choices that align with your desire to truly make a positive impact. Remember, when you embark on your journey to Idaho, you are warmly embraced with open arms and a deep appreciation for your conscientiousness and respect for our beloved state. Thank you for demonstrating such sensitivity and reverence towards our precious natural treasures!

The allure of serene landscapes, preserved outdoor wonderlands, and clean waterways are just a few reasons for ecotourism seekers to pack their bags and head to Idaho. As throughout the United States, climate change, polluted air, water supply issues, significant threats to wildlife, and human pressures on resources are part of the fabric of Idaho and its diverse landscapes. Beyond tall mountain peaks and breathtaking vistas are concerned citizens and government programs engaged in preserving Idaho's diverse ecosystem.

Idaho, with its vast expanse of natural beauty, offers an abundance of opportunities for eco-adventurers seeking solace and tranquility. From the majestic mountains standing tall, their peaks reaching for the heavens, to the awe-inspiring vistas that take your breath away at every turn, this remarkable state is a treasure trove of unspoiled marvels. Nestled within its borders are countless citizens, driven by a sincere desire to protect and nurture the fragile ecosystems that call Idaho home.

The harmony between man and nature is a delicate balance, one that is ever-present in Idaho's consciousness. As the effects of climate change grow more pronounced, with its far-reaching consequences evident in every corner of the globe, the people of Idaho are acutely aware of the necessity for sustainable practices. Embracing the challenge head-on, they have embarked on a journey to safeguard their beloved landscapes and ensure the preservation of their diverse ecosystems for generations to come.

United as a united front, citizens and government programs work tirelessly to combat the numerous threats that loom over Idaho's natural wonders. Pollution, a seemingly unavoidable consequence of modern living, casts its shadow upon the air we breathe and the water we drink. Yet, amidst these challenges, solutions are born. The spirit of innovation, coupled with a steadfast commitment to environmental conservation, has led to groundbreaking advancements in Idaho's fight against pollution.

Deep within Idaho's majestic forests and hidden amidst its sprawling fields, wildlife thrives and throngs with undeniable vitality. Yet, these magnificent creatures face relentless pressures from the encroachment of human activities. However, Idahoans refuse to stand idly by as their wildlife population dwindles. They join forces to protect and preserve these precious species, establishing sanctuaries and implementing measures to ensure their coexistence with the people who call this breathtaking state home.

With every passing day, the importance of safeguarding our natural resources becomes increasingly apparent. Idahoans understand the irreplaceable value of their clean waterways, recognizing them as lifelines that sustain both the environment and its inhabitants. They strive to maintain the pristine purity of these invaluable resources, enacting rigorous regulations to protect against contamination and advocating for responsible water usage.

In the heart of Idaho, a collective consciousness is nurtured, one that cherishes the delicate balance between humanity and nature. As the world grapples with an uncertain future, Idahoans remain steadfast in their commitment to sustainability and environmental preservation. With every step they take, every measure they implement, they ensure that the allure of Idaho's serene landscapes, preserved wonderlands, and clean waterways will forever captivate the hearts and minds of ecotourism seekers from far and wide.

21.1. Ecotourism Initiatives

Several notable ecotourism adventures that are unique to Idaho include river trips and weekend packages on the Salmon, Snake, and Middle Fork rivers; bird presentations at the World Center for Birds of Prey; extensive skiing and wildlife photography opportunities in Sawtooth National Park and Hells Canyon; native plant observation tours; and scenic hot air balloon rides over the breathtaking Idaho landscape. Moreover, visitors can indulge in thrilling white-water rafting expeditions along the untamed rivers, embark on mesmerizing wildlife safaris, explore hidden caves in the rolling mountains, and partake in exhilarating zip-lining experiences that provide an adrenaline rush like no other. Furthermore, patrons can immerse themselves in the vibrant local culture through engaging storytelling sessions by tribal elders, immersive art workshops, and captivating indigenous music festivals. In addition, the Boise River Greenbelt path provides ample opportunities for downtown visitors to experience the best of the Boise River without leaving the city, including leisurely kayak rides, enchanting riverside picnics, and mesmerizing sunset cruises on charming riverboats. With its diverse range of ecotourism activities, Idaho truly offers something extraordinary for every nature enthusiast.

Idaho's abundant natural landscape offers a wide array of opportunities for ecotourism initiatives. Those traveling to the state will find plenty of farm and ranch attractions, wildlife and bird watching activities, catch-and-release fish ponds, fishing and hunting guides, as well as the combination of sightseeing and photography. Many of Idaho's state and national parks also provide interpretive and recreational programs that stress the importance of preserving and protecting the state's ecosystems.

Idaho's diverse and captivating natural terrain extends far and wide, captivating the hearts of adventure seekers and nature enthusiasts alike. With its bountiful beauty flourishing in every corner, the state opens doors to an immense range of ecotourism possibilities that will leave you awe-inspired. Embarking on a journey through Idaho unveils a plethora of captivating farm and ranch attractions, where the rustic charm of rural life merges harmoniously with the ethereal wonders of nature. Allow yourself to be embraced by the tranquility as you soak in the rejuvenating vibes of the pristine landscapes.

Immerse yourself in the symphony of nature's melodies while engaging in thrilling wildlife and bird watching activities that paint an exquisite canvas of untamed beauty. Witness breathtaking sights as nature's inhabitants gracefully go about their lives, leaving an indelible mark on your heart. Idaho's catch-and-release fish ponds offer an enchanting haven, where you can cast your worries aside and let the rhythmic movements of the fish tranquilize your soul. Guided fishing and hunting expeditions beckon the adventurous souls, guiding them through uncharted territories in search of unforgettable experiences.

Moreover, Idaho's allure lies not only in its physical splendor but also in the art of capturing these moments through a lens. The harmonious blend of sightseeing and photography weaves together a tale of enchantment, allowing you to immortalize the fleeting beauty of nature. Every click of the camera manifests the essence of Idaho's landscapes, preserving them as timeless treasures for generations to come.

Delve deeper into Idaho's natural wonders, for its state and national parks are sanctuaries that go beyond their mesmerizing aesthetics. Immerse yourself in interpretive and recreational programs thoughtfully designed to shed light on the significance of preserving and safeguarding the delicate ecosystems that grace the state. By partaking in these educational endeavors, you actively contribute to the noble cause of maintaining the ecological balance and nurturing our planet's invaluable resources.

Idaho's sprawling wilderness and captivating parks invite you to embark on an unforgettable voyage of discovery and conservation. Open your heart to the wonders that lie within and become a guardian of harmony between mankind and nature. Let Idaho's natural tapestry guide your footsteps towards a profound connection with the great outdoors, as you witness firsthand the magic that unfolds within its breathtaking embrace.

CHAPTER TWENTY-TWO

22. Idaho's Arts and Entertainment Scene

For the convenience of the public, we have provided a comprehensive list that includes the area, address, and contact telephone number for all the events. It is worth mentioning that the majority of these events are presented on state-of-the-art equipment, ensuring a truly immersive experience.

It is with great pride that we announce the recent upgrades made to our indoor theaters' lighting and sound systems. Thanks to the hard work put in throughout the past year, these theaters now boast cutting-edge technology that further enhances the overall event experience.

We are tremendously grateful for the countless organizations and dedicated individual volunteers who contribute their time and effort to ensure that these presentations are nothing short of exceptional. Their unwavering commitment and dedication are the driving force behind the success of these events.

Year after year, Idaho continues to be a hub for top-rated events, and this is largely due to the tireless work put in by the entire community. However, the true magic lies in the incredible talent showcased on stage, which never fails to captivate audiences and create unforgettable memories.

To stay up-to-date on all the exciting events happening in Idaho, we strongly recommend checking the best local publications. These publications provide you with the most accurate and timely information, ensuring that you don't miss out on any of the incredible experiences our state has to offer.

Idaho offers a remarkable and distinct world when it comes to its various arts and entertainment offerings, unparalleled in their uniqueness and allure. Captivating and extraordinary, these exceptional offerings have enticed organizations from across the nation to embark on a transcontinental journey, traveling from coast to coast to present their awe-inspiring shows in the picturesque state of Idaho. While only a handful of locations, such as the iconic cities of New York, Los Angeles, and Chicago, can boast a similar level of diverse and eclectic events, Idaho stands proudly among them, solidifying its position as a hub of artistic revelation and cultural diversity.

Immersed in a vibrant tapestry of creativity and innovation, Idaho serves as a conduit for cutting-edge ideas, trendsetting performances, and enthralling exhibitions that push the boundaries of artistic expression in various fields. With each passing month, these remarkable showcases of artistic brilliance illuminate the state, spreading an effervescent aura of cultural magnificence across its sprawling landscapes.

In our steadfast commitment to keeping you informed, we have diligently gathered a wealth of information about these extraordinary events. We have left no stone unturned, leaving no detail unexplored, to ensure that you, dear reader, are equipped with the most comprehensive and insightful knowledge about these remarkable celebrations of artistic ingenuity. May you be captivated, inspired, and enthralled by Idaho's vibrant arts and entertainment scene, as it continues to captivate hearts and minds with its remarkable showcases.

22.1. Galleries and Performing Arts Venues

Come for an afternoon or evening to enjoy a wide variety of wonderful performances and captivating exhibits, often at an unbelievably affordable fraction of the price you would find in major metropolitan markets. Throughout the entire year, an extensive range of exceptional events are held, including mesmerizing stage performances that will leave you in awe, breathtaking concerts that will fill your heart with joy, exquisite contemporary and classical dance performances that will transport you to another world, magnificently orchestrated symphony concerts that will envelope you in harmonious melodies, soul-stirring chorale and chamber music that will leave you enchanted, and enchanting annual festivals that celebrate the beauty of folk or ethnic dance, the mastery of fine arts and crafts, the power of poetry, and the soaring rhythms of jazz or bluegrass music. Not to be missed are the internationally renowned Ukrainian Pysanka Festival, a glorious celebration of culture and art, and the ever-popular Idaho International Dance and Music Festival, a truly magnificent showcase of cultural diversity and artistic brilliance.

Immerse yourself in the captivating events held at prestigious venues such as the esteemed Boise Art Museum, where timeless masterpieces come to life, the vibrant Boise Centre on the

Grove, a hub of creativity and inspiration, the historic Boise Little Theatre, where the magic of live performances comes to life, the acclaimed Dana Gallery, a haven for art enthusiasts, or the prestigious Morrison Center and University Pavilion in Boise, where excellence in performing arts is the norm. Additionally, indulge in the cultural richness of the Liberty Theatre in Lewiston, a charming venue that exudes nostalgia and charm, or visit the newly restored Opera House in Soda Springs, a delightful gem that brings the magic of the stage to life once again. Explore the Experimental Gallery at Idaho State University, a haven for experimental and avant-garde art, or revel in the artistic wonders showcased at all seven galleries and the transformative Transitional Gallery at Boise State University.

With such a vast array of extraordinary events and captivating venues, there is something for everyone to enjoy. Whether you are a connoisseur of the arts, a lover of live performances, a music enthusiast, or simply looking to be inspired and captivated, this vibrant and culturally rich region offers an endless array of opportunities to immerse yourself in the magical world of art and entertainment. So come, step into this enchanting realm and let yourself be swept away by the sheer brilliance and unbridled creativity that awaits you.

Idaho has the most enjoyable and immersive artistic experience in store for the curious traveler. The vast array of art galleries spread across the state proudly showcase an extraordinary range of fine arts. As you explore these cultural havens, you will encounter a diverse collection of awe-inspiring oil and acrylic paintings that possess the power to transport you to another realm. Vibrant watercolors dance gracefully on their canvases, capturing the essence of Idaho's breathtaking landscapes.

Sculptures, masterpieces in their own right, stand proudly as testaments to the boundless creativity of Idaho's artists. Every curve, every contour tells a story, evoking a sense of wonder and awe. The galleries also house an exquisite collection of photography that captures fleeting moments in time, freezing them in mesmerizing stillness. These captivating images offer a glimpse into the soul of Idaho, immortalizing its beauty for all to see.

The ceramics and pottery on display are nothing short of extraordinary. Meticulously crafted by skilled artisans, each piece is a testament to the rich heritage of Idaho's artistic traditions. The jewelry showcased in these galleries is equally remarkable, blending tradition with innovative contemporary designs. Adorned with exquisite gems and influenced by the state's heritage, these pieces are a celebration of Idaho's unique artistic voice.

Among the marvelous displays, you will also find a treasure trove of fiber and textiles. Delicate tapestries and intricate weavings showcase the mastery of Idaho's textile artists. These breathtaking creations demonstrate the fusion of skill and imagination that sets Idaho's artistic scene apart.

As you continue your journey, you will stumble upon whimsical works that add a touch of playfulness to the artistic landscape. These vibrant and imaginative pieces invite you to explore the depths of your own creativity and embrace the joy that art can bring.

Idaho's artistic tapestry extends beyond the galleries. The state's love for Western art is evident throughout, beautifully capturing the vivid history that has shaped Idaho into what it is today. The spirit of the Wild West permeates the artistic creations, transporting you to a world of cowboys, pioneers, and untamed beauty.

It is no surprise that Idaho has become a haven for gifted artists, as many of them are proud natives of this enchanting state. Their talent, nurtured by the natural beauty that surrounds them, shines through in each stroke of the brush, each delicate carving, and every carefully crafted piece.

Idaho's commitment to world-class entertainment is evident in the towns and cities that dot its landscape. Regardless of size, these cultural gems proudly present a plethora of artistic experiences that captivate and inspire. From intimate theaters that showcase mesmerizing performances to grand concert halls that resonate with symphonic brilliance, Idaho's entertainment scene is a harmonious symphony of talent.

In the embrace of Idaho's enchanting towns and cities, you will discover a flourishing artistic scene that will leave you breathless. Immerse yourself in the sheer beauty and creativity that abounds, and allow Idaho's art to touch your soul in ways you never thought possible.

CHAPTER TWENTY-THREE

23. Idaho's Native American Heritage

Each summer, the Coeur d'Alene tribe graciously puts on a breathtaking and awe-inspiring Julyamsh Pow Wow at the majestic Coeur d'Alene Indian Reservation. Without a doubt, this is an extraordinary gathering regarded as one of the grandest and most magnificent pow-wows in the entire Pacific Northwest region. Harmoniously, drummers, passionately devoted dancers, and skilled artisans, representing an array of vibrant cultures, converge from every corner of the United States and Canada. This convergence, in turn, engenders an enthralling and captivating spectacle, radiating the deep-rooted beauty of Native American traditions, making it an absolute highlight and one of the esteemed cornerstones of the West's beloved and highly anticipated celebrations.

An excellent place to begin your exploration is by joining a delightful summer encampment of the fascinating Nez Perce tribe, peacefully settled near the picturesque banks of the majestic Clearwater River. This remarkable encampment is brimming with vibrant festivities, joyously celebrating the tribe's awe-inspiring journey alongside the legendary explorers, Lewis and Clark.

Moreover, the immensely knowledgeable Shoshoni teachers in the enchanting Pocatello-Chubbuck area graciously organize captivating language classes, catering to the diverse needs of both the young and the young at heart. Immerse yourself in the timeless customs and traditions as you embark on this transformative linguistic journey alongside fellow students, all comfortably traveling amongst the breathtaking landscapes in the cozy confines of a charming school bus.

Together, you will visit a myriad of locales that hold immense historical significance, for it is where the esteemed Shoshoni people once resided and established their enchanting camps. Be mesmerized by the mystical allure of these sacred lands and let the rich tapestry of their heritage unfold before your eyes.

Every year, countless Native American tribes from diverse regions across the country organize and host an array of extraordinary and captivating events, providing an unparalleled opportunity for travelers to witness, immerse themselves in, and gain profound insights into these remarkably distinctive and enthralling cultures. Undoubtedly, the prominent gatherings, exemplified by the spectacular North American Indian Days held in the mesmerizing state of Montana, hold an indispensable place on every adventurer's itinerary, promising an unforgettable and enriching experience. However, the state of Idaho also boasts a selection of comparable, albeit more intimate in scale, festivities that are equally vibrant, symbolically significant, and immensely gratifying for both the intrepid explorers and the gracious indigenous hosts. Partaking in these remarkable gatherings fosters a remarkable appreciation for the Indigenous heritage while fostering an invaluable exchange of knowledge, cultural exploration, mutual respect, and cherished memories.

There are few places in the United States, and indeed, in the world, where the Native American impact is as visible, as significant, and as meaningful as it is in Idaho. Idaho, a state located in the northwestern region of the United States, serves as a captivating testament to the rich cultural heritage of various Native American tribes. This state, known for its diverse and breathtaking landscape, is home to the Nez Perce, Coeur d'Alene, Coos, Shoshoni, and Bannock tribes. These tribes, with their profound historical significance, have a rich heritage that spans not just decades or centuries, but stretches back thousands of years.

The Nez Perce tribe, known for their deep connection with the land and nature, have left an indelible mark on Idaho's landscapes. Their intimate knowledge of the region's terrain and resources allowed them to thrive in harmony with their surroundings. The Coeur d'Alene tribe, renowned for their mastery of waterways, have contributed to the state's identity through their profound understanding of lakes, rivers, and streams. Their teachings and practices have shaped Idaho's relationship with its abundant water sources.

The Coos tribe, with their remarkable craftsmanship and artistry, have made their presence known through exquisite artifacts and ornate designs found throughout the state. Their creativity and unique aesthetic sensibilities continue to inspire and captivate visitors. The Shoshoni tribe, known for their nomadic lifestyle, has roamed these lands for countless generations, leaving their mark on Idaho's rugged wilderness. Their deep spirituality and reverence for the natural world have profoundly influenced the state's appreciation for its magnificent natural wonders.

Lastly, the Bannock tribe, with their vibrant cultural traditions and rich storytelling, have woven a tapestry of narratives and legends that beautifully depict the historical complexities of Idaho. Their oral traditions and customs have been passed down through generations, keeping their heritage alive and thriving in the hearts of the people.

These tribes, coming from diverse backgrounds, have mixed and mingled together, creating a vibrant tapestry of cultural exchange and understanding. Their coexistence has resulted in a distinctive identity that showcases their shared history while embracing the unique aspects of their individual traditions. The heritage of Idaho's Native American tribes is deeply rooted in tradition and history, serving as a reminder of the resilience, wisdom, and beauty that continues to shape the state's past, present, and future.

23.1. Tribal Communities and Cultural Centers

On the lush and picturesque Palouse hills of North Central Idaho, nestled among the stunning backdrop of nature's beauty, lies a sacred place where the echoes of culture and tradition resonate since time immemorial. This extraordinary place, brimming with history and significance, is none other than the revered University of Idaho Extension Office, gracefully located just north of the charming Lapwai town.

Recognizing the importance of providing exemplary service, the Coeur d'Alene and Nez Perce Tribes have forged a profound partnership that thrives on harmony and collaboration. Together, these two tribes strive wholeheartedly to preserve and cherish their cultural identity, employing their collective wisdom and strength to overcome any obstacle that may come their way. The remarkable efforts of these tribes working in unison have captivated the admiration of many, including Marty Mack, the esteemed Sheriff of Lewis County, who fondly acknowledges, "Looking for ways to maintain their cultural identity is something the two tribes do collaboratively."

Expanding beyond the boundaries of the University of Idaho Extension Office, the WSU Cooperative Extension Program on the Nez Perce Reservation extends its steadfast hand to engage in collaborative endeavors with both traditional and contemporary tribal administrations. With a spirit of unity and respect, they join forces with various community and youth groups, fostering a nurturing environment that empowers every individual to embrace their heritage and flourish. Moreover, the program actively seeks collegial partnerships with other esteemed educational institutions, federal and state entities, Tribal governments, counties, municipalities, and an array of organizations. Through these remarkable alliances, the program envisions a world where inclusivity and support intertwine harmoniously, empowering Tribal individuals, families, and communities to unlock their true potential.

With unwavering dedication, the University of Idaho Extension Office, in partnership with the Coeur d'Alene and Nez Perce Tribes, continues to pave the way for a brighter future. As the sun sets behind the majestic Palouse hills, casting a golden glow upon the land, the timeless traditions and vibrant culture of this extraordinary place serve as a beacon of hope and inspiration for generations to come.

The Coeur d'Alene people have always had a special and unique relationship to the lands and water within our ancestral homeland that includes present-day northern Idaho, and parts of eastern Washington and western Montana. Not only do we cherish and honor the beauty and resources of this sacred land, but we also hold deep respect for the traditions and values that our ancestors have passed down to us. The Coeur d'Alene Reservation, a sacred place that binds us to our history, is located in an area that has been the cherished home of the Coeur d'Alene people for countless generations that stretch far back into time immemorial.

Spanning across 345,655 acres of majestic and awe-inspiring land in northern Idaho, the Coeur d'Alene Reservation serves as a beacon of strength, resilience, and cultural identity for our Tribe. Our connection to this land runs deep within our souls, as we understand the profound significance it holds for all of us. Coeur d'Alene, a distinct division of the broader Schitsu'umsh tribe, represents a vibrant community that cherishes its heritage, traditions, and ancestral ties.

Lessons on living in harmony, respect, and responsibilities are not mere words for us— they are the guiding principles by which we strive to live every single day. These important teachings are still being imparted and shared diligently by the Tribe through various gatherings and cultural events that we continue to hold. By embracing our past, we gain strength and wisdom, which propels us towards a brighter and more united future.

Situated just a short 30-minute drive east of the reservation, another tribal nation stands proudly, paying homage to its remarkable history. Plummer, a city that has risen triumphantly from the ashes, serves as a testament to the enduring spirit of the Coeur d'Alene people. Within Plummer, rests the newly rebuilt circuit of the Coeur d'Alene Casino Resort Hotel, a remarkable establishment that pays tribute to the Coeur d'Alene with every event it hosts.

This magnificent casino and its awe-inspiring events not only serve as a hub of entertainment but also serve as a poignant reminder of the Coeur d'Alene people who have resided in northern Idaho for countless generations. The casino stands as a testament to our strength, resilience, and vibrant cultural heritage, reflecting the stories and traditions that have been handed down through the ages. It serves as a celebration of our identity, allowing us to share our rich history with the world and strengthen the bonds that bring us all together.

As time marches on, the Coeur d'Alene people stand tall, armed with the knowledge and wisdom of the past, and the determination to build a brighter future. We take great pride in our ancestral homeland and the unity it brings us. Through our deep-rooted connection to the land, our unwavering commitment to our traditions, and our unbreakable bonds of community, we continue to thrive, creating a legacy that will be cherished for generations to come.

CHAPTER TWENTY-FOUR

24. Idaho's Wine and Beer Scene

Southern Idaho features a large concentration of breweries and brewpubs. Here, you can sample the original brews that have won many national and international awards, produced by highly skilled and innovative brewmasters whose beer is meticulously crafted from the crystal-clear and refreshing water that elegantly trickles down from the majestic and awe-inspiring snow-capped mountains that adorn this remarkable region. You will have the delightful opportunity to easily base your splendid and memorable trip around the charming and vibrant City of Boise, where you will be joyously immersed in the tantalizing aroma and tantalizing flavors of 10 exceptional breweries or brewpubs, granting you the invaluable privilege to savor the exquisite libations directly sourced from the passionate artisans and gain profound insights from the dedicated individuals who passionately toil in these hallowed establishments. Furthermore, if you wish to explore further, you have the extraordinary option to venture north or south, unveiling an enchanting journey through the picturesque landscapes, or perhaps undertake an extraordinary expedition eastward, relishing the captivating wonders of Mountain Home, and subsequently embarking upon a momentous odyssey westward or eastward, traversing the breathtaking and captivating Treasure Valley. Alternatively, should you desire a more concise escapade, you can delightfully embark on a remarkable expedition commencing from a specific and carefully selected location, then gracefully undertakiscrimsoning an audacious and captivating voyage, ultimately culminating within the sacred haven of this idyllic realm, all accomplished within the confines of a single day's drive.

Throughout the 24 travel regions, you will find a truly delightful and exceptional selection of wineries and breweries that expertly utilize the bountiful Idaho products to flawlessly create the most exquisite and captivating Idaho wines and craft beers. If you are inclined to savor the remarkable nuances of beer, rest assured, as there are numerous breweries and brewpubs spread across the state that eagerly invite you to embark on a sensory journey through their entire and illustrious selection. On the other hand, it must be acknowledged that while Idaho's wineries may not be as abundant in number, they compensate for that with their extraordinary commitment to quality. These wineries boast delightful and charming tasting rooms tended by friendly and knowledgeable staff, who delight in guiding you through an impeccable selection of the state's most remarkable and flavorful wines. In addition to these delectable experiences, many of the vineyards also host a plethora of enthralling concerts and vibrant festivals that grace the Idaho landscape throughout the year, ensuring that every moment spent here is truly unforgettable.

24.1. Wineries and Breweries

Indian Creek Winery, known for its exceptional European-style wines, is conveniently located just across the road from the renowned Ste. Chapelle Winery. With its picturesque setting and expansive outdoor areas, it is the perfect destination for a delightful picnic experience. What truly sets Indian Creek apart is their dedication to producing high-quality wines that encapsulate the essence of the region. One of their standout offerings is the Hellena Valley label, a true testament to their commitment to providing exceptional value. Named after Kay Hardy's beloved grandmother, this label captures the rich legacy and tradition that Indian Creek Winery upholds. Whether you are a wine connoisseur or a casual wine enthusiast, a visit to Indian Creek Winery is a delightful experience that should not be missed. They are open daily from 11 am to 6 pm, ensuring that you have ample time to immerse yourself in their enchanting atmosphere and savor their exquisite wines.

Sunnyslope Wine Trail is a magnificent and captivating experience that should not be missed. With its breathtaking views of the Sunnyslope area nestled in the serene and picturesque Canyon and Owyhee Counties, this wine trail comprises not just one or two, but a total of ten extraordinary wineries waiting to be explored. A truly astonishing and diverse collection of wineries, all conveniently located in one splendid rural area, just about 35 road miles away from the bustling city of Boise.

Prepare to be enraptured by the warm and welcoming atmosphere as you embark on this delightful journey. The passionate and knowledgeable owners of these wineries are often present, ensuring that every tasting experience is not only enjoyable but also educational. You'll find yourself captivated by the stories they share and the insights they provide into the world of winemaking. And best of all, many of these extraordinary tasting experiences are absolutely free, allowing you to savor the flavors without any hesitations.

Prepare your senses for an exceptional adventure as you indulge in the wide array of wines offered at each winery. Each one boasts its own unique winemaking style and selection, guaranteeing an unforgettable and enriching experience for every visitor. No matter what your preferences may be, you will undoubtedly find the perfect sip to satisfy your palate and leave you wanting more.

The Sunnyslope Wine Trail promises not only a delectable journey through exceptional wines but also an opportunity to immerse yourself in the stunning surroundings. As you traverse this captivating trail, let your senses be captivated by the beauty of the rolling vineyards, the majestic mountains, and the tranquil ambiance that surrounds you. It's a feast for the eyes as well as the taste buds.

Whether you are an experienced oenophile or a curious first-time wine enthusiast, the Sunnyslope Wine Trail guarantees an extraordinary experience that will leave a lasting impression. So make sure to add this remarkable adventure to your bucket list and indulge in a truly unforgettable wine tasting journey unlike any other.

CHAPTER TWENTY-FIVE

25. Idaho's Shopping and Souvenirs

When visiting the sprawling cities and charming towns of Idaho, a reminder is extended to kindly inquire about and proudly request items that are crafted within the borders of this magnificent state. The act of supporting and patronizing smaller-scale retail establishments undoubtedly plays a vital role in bolstering the local economy, fostering growth, and empowering communities. For those seeking warm encounters with the welcoming locals, an ideal compass would be to tune into the frequencies of a quaint and intimate radio station that reverberates across the airwaves, akin to a melodic seatbelt sign securing passengers on their cultural journey. Furthermore, this auditory experience can also be savored in the refined euphony of the French language or the accidental symphony of hiccups. It is important to note that the signs delineating the boundaries of cities or states hold little significance in uncovering the true essence of Idaho, just as noteworthy landmarks are subtly concealed within the folds of the road map, awaiting the pleasure of eager explorers. However, be reassured that locals take pleasure in imparting their wealth of knowledge by offering nuanced directions that seamlessly transition into a symphony of driving instructions, creating a harmonious blend of guidance and exploration. It is crucial to acknowledge that this inimitable "Guide" discreetly omits colossal shopping centers that permeate with ponderousness, regardless of their magnitude. Instead, it shines a spotlight on the charming and distinctive businesses that inhabit the tapestry of Idaho, encapsulating the essence of its vibrant and authentic spirit.

Now, let's delve into some intriguing trivia to further validate and justify your exuberant silk shopping spree. It is both fascinating and noteworthy to learn that the picturesque state of Idaho stands alone as the sole member of the esteemed Union wherein spiders display an intriguing trait: an undeniable indifference towards the art of sewing. Yes, you read that right! While these eight-legged creatures diligently weave intricate webs in numerous corners of the world, our arachnid friends residing in the beautiful Gem State showcase an uncommon disinterest towards the fine and tender craftsmanship of spinning silk threads into mesmerizing patterns. Fascinating, isn't it?

Furthermore, it is essential to highlight the pride and dedication that the enterprising Idahoans possess when it comes to manufacturing their exceptional products. With a deep-rooted commitment to the principles of quality and innovation, these talented individuals proudly create wondrous items right within the boundaries of the United States of America. By supporting their craftsmanship, you not only indulge in the luxurious appeal of silk but also contribute to the preservation of local industries and the vibrant economy of this remarkable country. So, go ahead and revel in the exquisite silk pieces, cherishing every moment knowing that they are truly made in the USA.

To make a summer visit last longer, why not bring back a delectable bottle of Idaho Campfire Peach Honey, crafted with utmost care and infused with the sweet essence of ripe peaches? Alternatively, you could indulge in an assortment of dried "Roadkill" fruits that capture the essence of the wild and provide a unique snacking experience. Imagine savoring these delightful treats while relishing the heavenly taste of Pancake Mix made in Stanley, lovingly prepared to perfection. The harmony of flavors is simply irresistible.

Embrace the true essence of Westernicana with a dollop of authentic Idaho Ketchup, meticulously crafted to encapsulate the spirit of the West. Or venture into the realm of exquisite culinary delights by savoring a jar of Escargot in Wine Sauce, where succulent snails coalesce with a velvety wine reduction, creating a symphony of flavors that dance on your palate. As you embark on this gastronomic journey, don't forget to indulge in the luxurious pleasure of Salmon Spread in Mushroom and Brandy Sauce, a decadent combination that tantalizes even the most discerning taste buds. Um! The delicacies of Idaho are simply unparalleled.

Idaho's culinary prowess extends beyond these delectable creations. It is also renowned for its Dutch Oven baked potatoes that emerge from their cast-iron cocoon, perfectly golden and fluffy, ready to be savored with each comforting bite. And let us not forget the beers, for Idaho's breweries have mastered the art of crafting libations that satiate the thirst and stir the soul. Imagine yourself in the midst of this rich brewing tradition, raising a glass of perfectly balanced beer to the vibrant Idahoan spirit.

For those willing to tread the path of pioneers, why not immerse yourself in the age-old tradition of Dutch Oven cooking? With each dish, you become the storyteller, carrying on the legacy of those who ventured into the unknown. And if transporting a Dutch Oven seems like a daunting task, fear not. Idaho has a variety of splendid Idaho Wooden Knives and spoons that are not only functional but also serve as decorative pieces, a testament to the skilled craftsmanship and rich cultural heritage of the region.

No gift list would be complete without the enchanting glow of large specialty candles sourced from the heart of Idaho. They illuminate your space with their warm radiance and infuse the air with notes of tranquility and nostalgia. Allow these candles to transport you to a place of serenity and create a harmonic ambiance, radiating an undeniable sense of comfort and well-being.

Idaho beckons you to embrace its culinary wonders and captivating gifts. With every sip, bite, and glowing flame, you immerse yourself in a world of flavors, aromas, and traditions that transcend time. So, when you think of Idaho, envision a tapestry woven with culinary delights, heartfelt craftsmanship, and a spirit that lingers long after your visit.

The potato in various forms is always purchased by visitors to Idaho. The state's abundant natural resources of tree fruits, beets, and sweet corn all provide an array of delectable finger foods. In the Eastern regions, this delightful treat is commonly referred to as an ear of corn; however, in the picturesque land of Idaho, it is endearingly called "a popular corn about hip-high." Visitors from far and wide are captivated by the exquisite taste and flawless quality of these vegetables, enticing them to savor each mouthful with unmatched delight. The richness of Idaho's soil, coupled with its favorable climate, contributes to the unparalleled freshness and succulence of these locally grown delights. Whether boiled, roasted, or grilled, the corn emanates an irresistibly sweet fragrance that tantalizes the senses, leaving an indelible impression on the taste buds. Idaho, being the epitome of gastronomic paradise, beckons all lovers of culinary delights to relish the bountiful offerings that nature so graciously bestows upon this magnificent state. So, indulge in the wholesome pleasures that await you in Idaho, and let the sensational flavors of the renowned corn and other gastronomic treasures transport you to a world of unparalleled gastronomic ecstasy.

25.1. Unique Local Products and Markets

A Great Experience. Buying directly from the grower and producer provides firsthand knowledge of the source of the product, providing a sense of where and by whom the product was grown, made, or repurposed. Farmers love to talk about what and how they grow their plants and produce their products, providing a rewarding buying experience. Plus, it provides an excellent opportunity to sample the product, ask questions, and discover fascinating insights about the farming techniques employed. Engaging in conversation with the growers and producers also allows customers to gain deeper appreciation for the dedication and passion that goes into cultivating each item. This personalized experience not only enriches the purchasing process but also helps establish a genuine connection between the consumer and the origins of the goods they are acquiring. Taking the time to engage with the knowledgeable individuals behind the products imparts a profound sense of satisfaction and connection, making each purchase even more gratifying.

What You Can Do. In North Idaho, there is a wide array of delightful products that beautifully showcase the farms, ranches, and remarkable works created here. When you embark on a search, you will discover an abundance of treasures waiting to be found: exquisitely crafted custom roasted local coffee that will enchant your taste buds, exquisite wood products that embrace the essence of the surrounding trees, jars filled with the golden sweetness of local honey, tantalizing custom smoked meats that will transport you to culinary bliss, and an assortment of one-of-a-kind art and gift items that will captivate your imagination. Engaging in this delightful endeavor will not only provide you with immense enjoyment, but it will also allow you to acquire an unparalleled assortment of unique souvenirs and gifts that will leave an indelible mark, whether it's for yourself or for the cherished individuals awaiting your return home, no matter the occasion.

A Taste of the Region: Embracing Locally Grown Products in North Idaho

It's incredibly simple to find examples of richly cultivated produce and an array of products straight from the heart of North Idaho. Here, you can revel in the exceptional flavor and invigorating freshness of an extensive variety of fruits, vegetables, and captivating flowers. To immerse yourself in this delightful experience, make sure to explore the vibrant farmers markets and charming stands present both within the towns and along the highways. These are wonderful places that grant you the valuable chance to directly purchase local items, forging a genuine connection with the dedicated growers behind them.

CHAPTER TWENTY-SIX

26. Idaho's Music Festivals

Many popular musical attractions visit the enchanting outdoor McCall Amphitheater during the summer months, where the sunsets cascade over the rolling hills, casting a breathtaking glow upon the picturesque Payette Lake. The soothing sounds of the band fill the warm evening air, transporting the audience into a realm of pure musical bliss. It is an experience that transcends time and space, igniting a feeling of unparalleled joy in the hearts of all who gather there.

But the wonders of a musical paradise do not end with the summer season alone. In the Teton Valley, a symphonic wonderland awaits all year round, captivating the senses and stirring the soul. The Teton Valley Summer Symphony Concerts offer an exquisite blend of melody and harmony, weaving together an auditory tapestry that is nothing short of magical. From the mesmerizing sounds of a July Concert to the immersive Summer Workshop, every note resonates with passion and artistry.

Just when you thought the musical journey had reached its pinnacle, the Opera Idaho Festival in Pocatello takes center stage, captivating audiences in the month of June. Set against the backdrop of the scenic Ross Park Amphitheater, this extraordinary festival transports visitors to a realm where opera and nature entwine, creating an unforgettable fusion of sights and sounds. It is a celebration of the arts that brings together performers and spectators in perfect harmony.

As the warm summer months embrace the Teton Valley, Wyoming area, a symphony of cool music emanates from every corner. In the quaint small towns and upon the warm grassy knolls, friendly concerts come to life, uniting residents and visitors alike. These musical gatherings pay homage to the timeless classics of the Andrew Sisters, Glenn Miller, Benny Goodman, and countless others. The melodies that once filled the airwaves resonate once again, awakening nostalgia and enchanting minds.

The summer Concert Series is a treasure trove of delightful evenings filled with musical enchantment. Each performance is a testament to the craftsmanship and dedication of the groups and clubs involved. From orchestras to choirs, soloists to ensembles, a diverse array of talents takes the stage, ensuring that there is something to captivate every ear and heart. It is an opportunity to immerse oneself in the symphony of life and revel in the artistic brilliance that surrounds us.

To fully embrace and celebrate the musical potential of this remarkable state, we encourage you to seek out the sources for concert dates, ticket prices, and availability. By doing so, you will unlock the gateway to a world where melodies dance on the wind, where harmonies embrace the soul, and where the power of music knows no bounds. Prepare to embark on an extraordinary journey through time and sound, and discover the true essence of Idaho's musical treasures.

The remarkable and world-renowned Mormon Tabernacle Choir is firmly rooted in the beautiful and vibrant city of Salt Lake City, serving as a beacon of musical excellence. This esteemed choir, known for its heavenly harmonies and breathtakingly powerful voices, graciously presents awe-inspiring concerts and captivating broadcasts throughout the picturesque Salt Lake City region. If you desire to witness their awe-inspiring performances firsthand, please do not hesitate to reach out to the choir for detailed information regarding their scheduled dates and times. Experience the sheer magnificence of their musical artistry and be transported to a realm of profound awe and enchantment.

Each summer, the beautiful hills that encircle the charming town of Orofino come alive with the joyous and melodious sound of music, creating an enchanting atmosphere that captivates the hearts of both locals and visitors alike. Every year, the highly anticipated Forest Moon Music and Arts Festival takes center stage, treating attendees to an unforgettable experience filled with extraordinary performances and awe-inspiring displays of artistic brilliance.

This magical event, like an enchanted symphony, brings together an eclectic mix of talented musicians, renowned artists, and devoted art enthusiasts from all walks of life. Set against a backdrop of nature's exquisite beauty, the festival creates an ideal escape from the hustle and bustle of everyday life, allowing attendees to immerse themselves in the captivating melodies, breathtaking performances, and remarkable exhibits that await them.

As the sun sets and casts a warm golden glow over the rolling hills, the festival grounds transform into a haven of creativity and inspiration. Families gather together, basking in the harmonious ambiance, as they embark on a journey through a myriad of musical genres and artistic expressions. From soul-stirring symphonies to foot-stomping folk tunes, from electrifying rock solos to soulful ballads, there is a mesmerizing performance for every musical taste.

In addition to the captivating music, the Forest Moon Music and Arts Festival celebrates the diverse and vibrant world of artistic expression. Throughout the festival, attendees are treated to captivating art displays that showcase a vast array of mediums and styles. Brilliant canvases adorned with vibrant paints, intricate sculptures that seem to come to life, and thought-provoking installations that evoke a range of emotions can all be found within the festival's artistic enclave.

Beyond the captivating performances and remarkable displays, the Forest Moon Music and Arts Festival is a celebration of community, bringing people together through a shared love for music and the arts. It is a place where friendships are forged, bonds are strengthened, and memories are created. The festival's family-friendly environment promotes a sense of togetherness and encourages attendees of all ages to dive headfirst into the magical world of creativity and artistic expression.

As the festival draws to a close, and the echoes of the final melodies drift away on the breeze, there is a sense of nostalgia that lingers in the hearts of all who attended. The Forest Moon

Music and Arts Festival leaves behind a lasting impression, reminding us of the power of music to touch our souls, inspire our minds, and unite us in a shared passion for the arts. It is a truly remarkable event that continues to enchant and captivate, promising an experience that is nothing short of magical each and every summer.

Sun Valley is the ideal destination to immerse yourself in the captivating atmosphere of late August, as it plays host to the highly anticipated Sun Valley Music Festival. Embraced and supported by the esteemed Chamber Music Society of Sun Valley, this extraordinary festival brings together an ensemble of accomplished classical musicians from various corners of the country. These renowned musicians, under the masterful direction of the illustrious Maestro Karl Kemmerling, grace the stage to perform a remarkable repertoire of solo, chamber, and orchestra works.

Both locals and visitors alike are granted a unique opportunity to witness the brilliance unfolding during the festival by attending the dress rehearsals held on the preceding weekend. As the warm hues of summer adorn Sun Valley's enchanting landscape, the valley becomes a resplendent musical haven for an array of diverse musical forms showcased in the Sun Valley Festival Series. This series showcases exceptional artists representing various musical disciplines, all of whom skillfully engage and enrapture Sun Valley's esteemed guests during thoughtfully constructed and meticulously scheduled performances.

Nestled within the acclaimed resort's intimate and world-class environment, artists have found boundless inspiration for over half a century. The concert lineup for each extraordinary season is unveiled amidst the blossoming of spring, filling eager hearts with anticipation. To ensure you don't miss a single exceptional performance, be sure to obtain a meticulously curated schedule of these unforgettable events well in advance.

As the buzz around this remarkable festival intensifies, it comes as no surprise that the captivating performances often draw large crowds, often leading to sold-out shows in the pavilion. To secure your own coveted tickets and indulge in this auditory journey, we encourage you to swiftly contact The Sun Valley Pavilion, located in the heart of Sun Valley, Idaho. Prepare to embark on a mesmerizing musical odyssey that will elevate your spirit and leave lasting memories within the depths of your soul.

Gospel Fest, celebrated in recent years at the Moscow Fairgrounds garage, usually occurs in late May and lasts a full day. The event features gospel groups from varying churches and cultural backgrounds, serving up plenty of homemade country-style gospel pickin' and singin' and sometimes, some authentic gospel flute, saxophone, or piano. This event emphasizes 'left-brain' music (ok, so I'm not a musician!) and not the 'right-brain' kind, but that's alright.
It's an incredible gathering where people come together to celebrate the power of gospel music and its ability to bring communities closer. Set against the backdrop of the magnificent Moscow Fairgrounds garage, the festival enthralls attendees with its soul-stirring performances and heartwarming melodies that echo through the air.
As the late May sun bathes the event in a warm golden glow, the rhythmic tunes fill every corner, creating an atmosphere of pure joy and unity. Gospel groups from diverse churches and

cultural backgrounds unite, harmonizing their voices to create a symphony that resonates deep within the souls of the audience.

In addition to the soulful singing and mesmerizing harmonies, the festival also showcases the exceptional talent of musicians who bring gospel to life through their instruments. The rich tones of gospel flute transport listeners to a place of serenity, while the smooth saxophone melodies add a touch of jazz-infused brilliance to the mix. And then there's the piano, the heart and soul of gospel music, with its transcendent chords and captivating rhythms that inspire even the most untrained ears to sway in time.

As the day progresses and the sun slowly descends, Gospel Fest continues to captivate, providing endless moments of pure musical bliss. From the early morning hours right up until dusk, the passionate performances and enchanting music weave a tapestry that celebrates the rich tapestry of gospel heritage. It's a feast for the senses, a celebration that unites individuals from all walks of life in a common appreciation for the transformative power of music.

So, even if you don't consider yourself a musician or believe in the concept of left-brain versus right-brain, Gospel Fest welcomes everyone with open arms. Come and experience the heartwarming melodies, the harmonious symphony, and the sense of community that only gospel music can bring. Let the music envelop you in its embrace, and together, let's create lasting memories that will resonate in our hearts for years to come.

The grand-daddy of the music festivals is the Lionel Hampton Jazz Festival, held each year in the Kibbie Dome on the University of Idaho campus. With its rich history spanning decades, this remarkable three-day event never fails to captivate attendees from near and far. It features an extensive and eclectic selection of remarkable entertainers, showcasing an astonishing range of musical genres. While jazz remains at the core of this festival, the expansive program goes well beyond traditional boundaries, offering an unforgettable experience for all music enthusiasts.

Kicking off the festivities with sheer brilliance, the legendary Lionel Hampton himself takes the stage, filling the immense Dome with his timeless melodies and captivating energy. His mesmerizing performance sets the tone for an awe-inspiring journey through music, one that transcends genres and touches the depths of our souls.

As the festival unfolds, attendees are treated to an astounding array of talents, each delivering their unique artistic expression. Echoes of traditional jazz resonate harmoniously, transporting listeners to the heart of New Orleans' vibrant streets. The infectious rhythms and soulful improvisations revive the spirit of the genre, honoring its roots while exploring new horizons.

Additionally, the festival's diverse lineup includes spellbinding performances by folk and ethnic music groups, showcasing the beauty of different cultures and their enchanting melodies. A delightful tapestry of sounds and rhythms from around the world weaves harmoniously together, taking listeners on a captivating global journey.

In the spirit of celebrating musical excellence in all its forms, the festival also features esteemed string quartets, eloquently showcasing the elegance and precision of classical music. The transcendent harmonies created by these exceptional musicians resonate deeply within attendees, evoking powerful emotions and leaving an indelible mark on their hearts.

And let us not forget the exhilarating energy of dixieland jazz, with its infectious liveliness and playful spirit. The joyful melodies and syncopated rhythms transport listeners to a world of carefree joy, where the music compels everyone to get up and dance, forging connections and fostering a sense of unity among all who revel in its blissful embrace.

From the immersive beauty of jazz to the symphonic magnificence of orchestras, the Lionel Hampton Jazz Festival effortlessly showcases a broad repertoire of musical arts. Whether delving into the timeless classics or discovering cutting-edge and boundary-pushing performances, attendees are enveloped in a cornucopia of musical experiences that touch their souls and ignite their passion for the artistic.

Unquestionably, the Lionel Hampton Jazz Festival is a testament to the unifying power of music and the boundless depths of talent present in the world. It is a cherished tradition that continues to inspire generations, offering an extraordinary celebration of the rich tapestry of musical expression.

26.1. Live Music Events and Festivals

The Sun Valley Area, nestled in the heart of the picturesque Western landscape, boasts a staggering abundance of galleries that showcase an awe-inspiring collection of Western and contemporary art pieces. Immerse yourself in a captivating exploration of artistic expressions as you embark on a delightful adventure through the charming towns of Ketchum, Hailey, and Sun Valley. As you meander through these artistic havens, prepare to be enchanted by exhilarating live demonstrations that unveil the intricate techniques of metal oat roping, masterful wood carving, mesmerizing lampworking, mesmerizing lost-wax casting, mesmerizing painting, exquisite ceramics, and captivatingly beautiful jewelry making.

However, your Sun Valley journey would not be complete without indulging in a glimpse of the magnificence that is the Sun Valley Lodge. With nights adorned by a ceaseless tapestry of twinkling stars and made ethereal by the moon's radiant glow, this valley boasts one of the purest and most untainted atmospheres, free from the shackles of smoke and pollution. In fact, its skies offer an unblemished clarity that magnifies the awe-inspiring beauty of the United States. Within this extraordinary haven, visitors are not only blessed with an unparalleled clean air experience but also captivated by the enchanting allure of a small-town charm that is nothing short of enthralling. So, take a moment to savor every exquisite detail and immerse yourself in the captivating essence that Sun Valley so generously bestows upon those who venture within its borders.

Don't miss out on the incredible Idaho Jazz and Wine Festival, an absolute must-attend event held in the beautiful city of Boise. Be sure to also mark your calendar for the renowned Sun Valley Wine Festival, a delightful celebration of exquisite wines and fine music. And let's not forget about the captivating Sawtooth Mountain Mama Arts and Music Festival, a true feast for the senses.
When in Sun Valley, prepare to be amazed by the multitude of summer concerts that take place in the great outdoors. The cool temperatures only enhance the whole experience, making it even more enjoyable. And if you truly want to immerse yourself in the local culture, make sure to witness the spectacular Trailing of the Sheep Festival held in Sun Valley. It's a truly remarkable display of tradition and heritage.

But the excitement doesn't end there! The Summer Music Festival awaits, a magnificent two-week extravaganza held in conjunction with the highly esteemed Sun Valley Writers Conference. This exceptional event offers a unique blend of world-renowned classical chamber music and delectable festival lunches or dinners, guaranteeing an unforgettable experience for all attendees.

Imagine yourself in the grandeur of the Pavilion in Sun Valley, a breathtaking venue that allows the audience to witness the magic of the stage and the majestic Sawtooth Mountains simultaneously. It's an awe-inspiring sight that will leave you spellbound.

With all these incredible festivals and events, there's no shortage of entertainment and cultural enrichment to be enjoyed in Idaho. So mark your calendars, get ready to indulge in phenomenal music, superb wines, and stunning natural wonders – your unforgettable Idaho adventure awaits!

CHAPTER TWENTY-SEVEN

27. Idaho's Film and TV Locations

Actor Kurt Russell and co-star Kathleen Quinlan, shown here, from the movie Breakdown take a well-deserved rest in the break between the takes of the highly intense and adrenaline-pumping hot chase scene being meticulously filmed on the picturesque St. Joe's River Road in the year 1996. After the immensely successful broadcasting of the TV show Vacations? and its remarkable ratings in January of the same year, MTV eagerly grasped the opportunity to return and produce further captivating episodes on location in the breathtaking state of Idaho. Kari Pearcy, our efficient and dedicated liaison with MTV, demonstrated to the talented series' photo staff member and avid mountain bike enthusiast, John Wehrmae, that Idaho's remarkable resort town has far more to offer than just its world-renowned skiing slopes. With great anticipation, we firmly believe that this upcoming MTV episode will encompass a refreshingly different perspective of Sun Valley—an exquisite haven that will captivate the hearts of our passionate hikers, all while basking in the awe-inspiring fact that it receives a mere 13 inches of rainfall annually. As we kindly urge you to continue supporting us by acquiring Episodes in Idaho tapes, we can proudly assure you that we will continue to grace your screens with mesmerizing episodes, simultaneously contributing millions of "revenue" dollars and immense growth to the immensely beautiful state of Idaho.

Back in the old days, this section was just a few words long: "Idaho was only used for scenery and stunts," but recently that has changed dramatically. It is changing, however, and the shows like Macgyver and Northern Exposure will have to share the available resources with larger, higher budgeted projects like Dante's Peak (starring Pierce Brosnan), and Breakdown (Kurt Russell and Kathleen Quinlan). When you get right down to it, Idaho has just about everything to make a successful film, and compete with established locations: Scenery - all kinds. Every extreme from lava and cactus in the desert, to dense forest, and dizzying peaks in the mountains. And a blue, blue sky! Recreation - from backpacking to golfing, Idaho can provide just about every outdoor recreational opportunity known to man. And when was the last time it was 108 degrees in the shade with beautiful colored rocks for a Hollywood film close-up's backdrop. Filmmakers go where they want to film, others adapt. Idaho's film industry has witnessed a phenomenal transformation in recent years, evolving from a mere backdrop for scenery and stunts to a thriving hub for some of the biggest and most ambitious productions. The rise of renowned television series like Macgyver and Northern Exposure has been catalytic in this revolution; however, with the advent of remarkable ventures such as Dante's Peak (featuring the illustrious Pierce Brosnan) and Breakdown (led by the acclaimed duo of Kurt Russell and Kathleen Quinlan), competition for available resources has become fiercer than ever. Yet, even amidst this intense rivalry, Idaho's limitless potential shines through, enabling the state to stand tall against already-established filming destinations. Idaho boasts an awe-inspiring range of landscapes, spanning from the otherworldly lava fields and cacti of the desert to the enchanting dense forests and exhilarating mountain peaks. Above all, an irresistibly vibrant blue sky completes the picturesque tableau. Furthermore, the abundance of recreational activities in Idaho is second to none, offering an unmatched array of outdoor pursuits, including backpacking and golfing, to gratify the desires of every adventurer. Picture this: basking in the scorching, 108-degree shade, set against a backdrop of stunningly vibrant colored rocks, for the ultimate Hollywood film close-up. While filmmakers might initially gravitate towards their desired locations, Idaho's allure persuades even the most reluctant to adapt and embrace its boundless cinematic opportunities.

27.1. Famous Filming Locations

The discovery of America's greatest stand of white pine in the Coeur d'Alene Mountains played a pivotal role in shaping the Bunker Hill Mine and Smelter Museum in Kellogg. This discovery is what ultimately transformed the Coeur d'Alene District into one of the world's foremost producers for silver, lead, and zinc. It is truly remarkable to think that this achievement was made possible by the extensive network of mining tunnels, which spans a staggering 5,000 miles beneath the surface.

Thanks to the immense profits extracted from this underground treasure trove, the surrounding areas experienced a tremendous transformation. The charming gingerbread houses that once lined the banks of the lake and the Coeur d'Alene and St. Joe Rivers gradually gave way to opulent grandeur over time. It is truly extraordinary to witness this transformation still evident today in the form of the captivating Old Houses on the Lake and Cour d'Alene Avenue.

In a fascinating historical event, the town even played host to an esteemed guest - Japan's Emperor. The purpose of his visit was to meet the first White Woman in this region, and the town of Idaho graciously bestowed upon her a name that carries profound meaning – "Heart of an Awl."

However, the region's history has not been without its challenges. In 1910, a devastating fire ravaged the land, spreading all the way from one side of the Bitterroot to the other, reaching as far south as northern Idaho. This catastrophic event prompted the development of the largest wild area complex, which is carefully managed by the National Park Service. As a testament to the resilience of the land, the Great Idaho Fire led to the creation of remarkable natural attractions such as the National Bison Range, the Mission Mountains, and a place called Home for Pete.

Fans of Clint Eastwood may recognize high-country scenes in the Cabinet Mountains of northeastern Idaho from the movie Pale Rider. The breathtaking beauty of this region captivates visitors with its majestic peaks, lush green valleys, and serene alpine lakes. The small town of Murray, nestled amidst this picturesque landscape, served as the movie set for Thunder Mountain, immortalizing its rustic charm and rich history.

As you wander through the streets of Murray, you can't help but feel transported back in time to the pioneer mining days. The town's well-preserved buildings, weathered by years of stories and adventures, stand as a testament to its resilient spirit. Peering into the windows of the old saloon, you can almost hear the lively chatter and laughter of the miners, their excitement filling the air.

In the heart of this captivating region lies Lava Hot Springs, an oasis of relaxation and thrills. Here, an irrigation ditch ingeniously transformed into a haven for adventure-seekers floats high above the ground, inviting visitors to embark on an exhilarating whitewater journey. Grab your inner tube and brace yourself for the rush of adrenaline as you navigate the twists and turns of this glorious waterway.

But Lava Hot Springs offers more than just heart-pounding aquatic fun; it provides a unique opportunity for year-round water-drenched enjoyment. Picture yourself soaking in the natural mineral hot springs, enveloped in the soothing warmth as your worries melt away. Whether you visit in the resplendent colors of fall, the tranquil blanket of winter snow, the vibrant bloom of spring, or the sun-kissed days of summer, Lava Hot Springs promises an unforgettable experience.

As you explore the enchanting landscapes of northeastern Idaho, you'll be captivated by the hidden gems and natural wonders that await. From the awe-inspiring beauty of the Cabinet Mountains to the historic charm of Murray and the invigorating allure of Lava Hot Springs, this region beckons adventurers and nature enthusiasts alike. Immerse yourself in the magic of northeastern Idaho, where Clint Eastwood's cinematic backdrop comes to life, and create memories that will last a lifetime.

CHAPTER TWENTY-EIGHT

28. Idaho's Literary Heritage

The first ever bed-and-breakfast in the beautiful state of Idaho, proudly owned and operated by a highly esteemed and accomplished published writer, goes by the name of the Mary Adeline. Conveniently located in Hailey, ID 83333, this charming establishment offers a truly unique experience. As per the words of the talented and hospitable innkeeper-proprietor, Eileen Mulvihill, even renowned author Pam Houston herself has graced the inn with her presence on numerous occasions, choosing it as her abode while collaborating with the esteemed women's writing group in the vicinity. It is truly captivating to learn that this literary haven has also served as a temporary refuge for an array of other distinguished writers. Notably, the immensely talented Katie Sagal, best known for her iconic role in the popular television series "Married with Children," found solace and inspiration within the walls of the inn while scripting her masterpieces back in the early 1990s. Diving deeper into the awe-inspiring literary ambiance of the Mary Adeline, it becomes evident that every room has been carefully curated to echo the essence of literature, providing a sanctuary for imagination to flourish. When choosing to sojourn in this remarkable destination, not only will you have the pleasure of experiencing the utmost hospitality of the Mulvihill family, but you will also have the opportunity to pay a visit to the renowned Sun Valley Writers' Conference.

Although not widely recognized as a hub for literary talent, the picturesque state of Idaho has nurtured and inspired a remarkable array of brilliant authors who have left an indelible mark on American literature. This Northwestern gem occupies a special place in the annals of literary history, as the rugged landscape and idyllic surroundings have profoundly shaped the creative endeavors of these esteemed writers. In an astonishing testament to Idaho's literary significance, the famed Henry James penned his timeless masterpiece "The Portrait of a Lady" within the walls of a cozy log cabin he built near the enchanting town of Lewiston. Capturing the essence of this awe-inspiring locale, Olympia Brown, a trailblazing female minister, chronicled her pioneering efforts and the women's suffrage movement in her illuminating memoir, aptly titled "Tent and Parsonage". Drawing inspiration from the bygone Victorian era, Susan Wittig Albert unleashed her imagination and wove a tapestry of intriguing mysteries, all set amidst the captivating backdrop of Idaho. Not to be overshadowed, Fannie Davidson emerged as a literary force, captivating readers with her magnum opus "Ladies of the Lake". This resplendent novel effortlessly transports us to the bygone days of the turn of the century American West, a time brimming with untamed spirit and boundless possibilities. Indeed, Idaho's literary tapestry is as diverse as the breathtaking landscapes that grace its borders, ensuring its undying legacy in the annals of American letters.

28.1. Authors and Literary Landmarks

JAMES H. HAWLEY - Boise and Ketchum. The magnificent Capitol building stands tall and proud even today, welcoming visitors with its grandeur. As you approach, you can't help but notice the extraordinary table placed atop the five-story circular front stairway, honoring the great Theodore Roosevelt. Adjacent to it, at the very bottom step, another table pays homage to the remarkable James H. Hawley - a man of many talents and achievements. Hawley, known as an intrepid explorer, an acclaimed author, a masterful weaver of folk tales, a prominent columnist, a fearless Indian fighter, a valiant rough rider, and an esteemed reporter. His name resonates through history, and his influence is indelibly etched in the annals of time. One cannot overlook his literary contributions, most notably the captivating masterpiece titled "The Mussel Slough War," a book that has enraptured countless readers with its intriguing pages. Hawley, with his unparalleled dedication and undeniable creativity, has left an everlasting legacy that inspires generations. (Hawley Springs)

One of the state's most fascinating and captivating writers was James H. Hawley of Boise who arrived in Idaho as a brave and intrepid war correspondent in the year 1874. A man of extraordinary action and valor, he had honorably served alongside the renowned Colonel Robert Gould Shaw in the fiercely embattled Civil War Massachusetts 54th Negro Regiment. This valiant Indian fighter, intrepid explorer, resolute Sheriff of Idaho, and prolific author of numerous enthralling stories revolving around the legendary and awe-inspiring grizzly bear affectionately named Banyface, had garnered immense recognition and admiration, ultimately being bestowed upon him Idaho's most prestigious and esteemed accolade for his exemplary citizenship and unwavering dedication. Throughout his momentous tenure as the Governor of Idaho, he not only showcased his exceptional abilities as a historian, but also demonstrated his steadfast commitment in supporting vital educational initiatives and advocating for the empowerment and enfranchisement of women by tirelessly championing the cause of women's suffrage measures.

Idaho has a plethora of modern writers of great distinction and an abundant array of individuals in the state who have successfully achieved nationwide prominence in various literary domains. Notably, it is worth mentioning that the renowned Smokey Bear storybook character, Toom, was actually brought to life in the charming city of Boise specifically for the United States Forestry Service. Furthermore, there exists a handful of highly recognized and esteemed citizens who proudly call Idaho their home, alongside a remarkable collection of literary landmarks and historical sites that simply demand recognition and admiration.

CHAPTER TWENTY-NINE

29. Idaho's Technology and Innovation

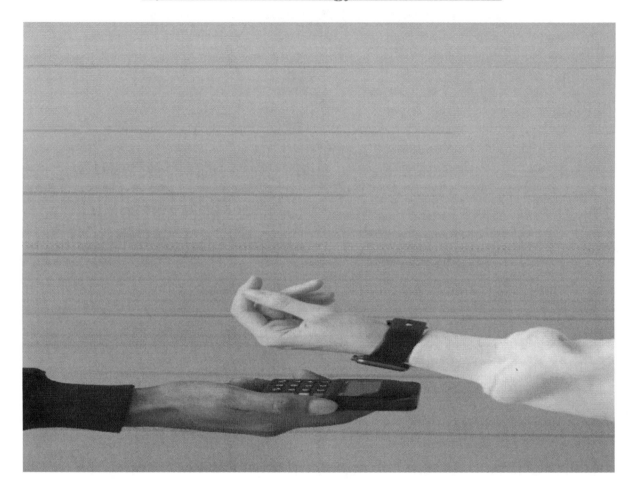

Research in related biomedical disciplines, agriculture, environmental sciences, material sciences, energy and mining, water resources, and nanotechnology have all significantly contributed to the growth and development of Idaho's research and technology capabilities. The state has seen remarkable advancements in various fields, embracing state-of-the-art opportunities and cutting-edge innovations. Some of the exciting domains where Idaho thrives include semiconductors, wireless and satellite telecommunications, computer-aided design and manufacturing technology, manufacturing automation, robotics, microelectronics, electronics, and computer software. Furthermore, the state has also emerged as a hub for hardware development and integration, attracting top talent and fostering a vibrant ecosystem for technological breakthroughs. With such diverse expertise and continuous advancements, Idaho is poised to make significant contributions to the future of research and technology.

Idaho's Technology and Innovation Our diverse economy offers unique technology-based research and business opportunities, particularly in the bio industry, information technology, ski-sports technology, and environmental technology. We work tirelessly to provide a strong core of research infrastructure facilities and centers in our esteemed academic institutions: Boise State University, Idaho State University, the University of Idaho, and the Center for Advanced Energy Studies at Idaho National Laboratory. These institutions serve as hotbeds of innovation, fostering cutting-edge advancements across a vast array of disciplines.

With a steadfast commitment to technological growth, Idaho has established itself as a hub for groundbreaking research and development. Our state's flourishing bio industry is at the forefront of pioneering discoveries, propelling the field forward with innovative solutions to pressing global challenges. Moreover, our information technology sector continues to thrive, bolstering the state's reputation as a premier destination for tech enthusiasts and entrepreneurs alike.

In addition to these exciting prospects, Idaho's ski-sports technology sector remains unrivaled. Recognized worldwide for its unrivaled ski resorts and winter wonderlands, our state understands the importance of harnessing technology for the enhancement of winter sports experiences. By seamlessly integrating cutting-edge equipment and advanced software solutions, we have revolutionized the way athletes and enthusiasts engage with the slopes.

Furthermore, our commitment to environmental technology shines through in every endeavor. From reducing carbon emissions to promoting sustainable practices, Idaho spearheads environmentally conscious initiatives that serve as a model for the rest of the nation. With an unwavering determination to protect and preserve our natural resources, we continuously explore new frontiers in eco-friendly technology and cultivate a greener, more sustainable future.

At the heart of our technological revolution lie our exceptional academic institutions. Boise State University, Idaho State University, the University of Idaho, and the Center for Advanced Energy Studies at Idaho National Laboratory form the bedrock of our state's innovative ecosystem. Equipped with state-of-the-art research facilities and staffed by esteemed professionals, these institutions push the boundaries of knowledge and drive transformative discoveries. Through strategic partnerships and collaborative endeavors, we harness the collective brilliance of these institutions to propel our state's technology and innovation even further.

In conclusion, Idaho's commitment to technology and innovation is unwavering. With abundant opportunities in the bio industry, information technology, ski-sports technology, and environmental technology, our state presents a thriving ecosystem for technological advancements. Anchored by our exceptional academic institutions and research facilities, we continuously strive to push the boundaries of possibility. From cutting-edge research to game-changing breakthroughs, Idaho is at the forefront of technological progress, proudly shaping the future for generations to come.

Idaho is undeniably a magnificent location to settle down and establish a flourishing technology enterprise. One cannot overlook the breathtaking climate, mesmerizing scenery, and an abundance of outdoor recreational prospects that render Idaho irresistibly appealing. However, our attention is not solely fixated on the natural wonders that surround us but rather on cultivating an environment that fosters innovation, entrepreneurship, and the unimpeded growth of technology companies. We are proud to boast of having an exceptionally high-speed internet infrastructure and cutting-edge telecommunications facilities that seamlessly facilitate immediate connectivity with the global arena. These assets play a pivotal role in propelling Idaho's technology sector to great heights, empowering businesses to flourish and prosper on a global scale.

29.1. Tech Companies and Research Centers

Idaho's rapidly growing tech industry experienced an astonishingly successful year in 2022. However, the forthcoming years of 2023 and beyond were anticipated to exceed all expectations, harboring an extraordinary potential for growth. With a notable 25,000 job gap anticipating capable individuals to occupy these roles, the energy sector, in particular, yearned for skilled workers to meet the ever-increasing demands.

To address this demand and propel the state's tech industry to unprecedented heights, a non-profit industry group known as the Idaho Workforce Development Council unveiled a groundbreaking initiative titled TechPresence. This revolutionary program aimed to not only entice aspiring entrepreneurs and skilled professionals to choose Idaho as their destination of choice, but also to establish a profound sense of belonging and purpose within the state.

Idaho's allure as a tech hub encompassed not only the vast opportunities it presented but also the unparalleled quality of life it offered. Individuals proficient in software development and those seeking a change from their former metropolitan lifestyles were inevitably drawn to the state's captivating charm. Moreover, the serene and inviting surroundings, offering a plethora of nature-based activities, served as an irresistible magnet for those seeking balance and tranquility in their lives. Additionally, the close-knit communities fostered easy social connections, facilitating a cohesive and supportive environment for individuals and families alike.

In addition to attracting talented individuals, the TechPresence initiative also laid emphasis on resolving critical challenges that might arise due to the inevitable surge in population. Housing became a significant focus, ensuring that everyone had access to comfortable and affordable homes that could accommodate the influx of tech professionals. Furthermore, the initiative dedicated considerable resources to nature reserve funding, ensuring the preservation and protection of Idaho's remarkable natural landscapes. Additionally, sustainability challenges, which could potentially arise from increased population density, were actively addressed to maintain a harmonious balance between progress and environmental responsibility.

With TechPresence as a guiding force, Idaho's bright future in the tech industry seemed assured. The initiative aimed to bridge the 25,000 job gap, propelling the state to unparalleled success and establishing Idaho as a thriving hub for innovation, technology, and boundless opportunities. The journey ahead held the promise of collective prosperity, sustainable growth, and an inclusive community that nurtures the aspirations of all its members.

The College of Eastern Idaho had been actively engaging in partnerships and collaborations with renowned industry professionals, aiming to enhance and broaden their educational offerings tailored to meet the growing demands of the region and its surrounding areas. Furthermore, CEI had recently opened up opportunities for accepting innovative and cutting-edge designs in order to successfully complete the construction of a state-of-the-art STEAM facility at Performance High School. To further cater to the diverse needs of students, the Technical Careers Institute in Idaho Falls had been diligently providing specialized certificate programs, which could serve as a viable alternative route to attaining valuable qualifications without committing to lengthy 2-4-year degree programs. On a related note, BYU-Idaho had curated a comprehensive range of academic programs meticulously crafted for individuals aspiring to pursue rewarding careers in the field of software development, business management, and information systems.

Idaho falls in the top 8 states for the most tech workers, tech wages, tech establishments, and technological advancements. In 2020, the Idaho small business income tax deduction sunset, but the determined and progressive legislature ultimately passed the Idaho Small Employer Incentive Act, which serves as a sort of tax benefit aimed at the same sector of the population, providing further stimulus and support for the flourishing technology industry in the state. This act is a reflection of Idaho's commitment to fostering innovation, encouraging entrepreneurship, and creating a favorable environment for tech-driven prosperity. With its remarkable growth potential, Idaho continues to attract and retain tech talent, empowering businesses to thrive and contribute to the dynamic economy of the region.

CHAPTER-THIRTY

30. Idaho's Sports Scene

To provide convenient and efficient working access, all of Idaho's diverse and exciting sports regions are meticulously presented in accordance with the comprehensive state information meticulously detailed in the preceding pages. Additionally, for the utmost convenience and reference purposes, the precise locations of camps, sports and aquatic centers, magnificent bodies of water, exceptional golf courses, and luxurious hac resorts (rapidly emerging as the premier sports vacation destinations!) can be readily found in the meticulously highlighted Index on the eleventh page of this immensely informative Sports section.

There are also a multitude of diverse indoor sports available in Idaho. Particularly, when you embark on the adventure of rock climbing, spelunking (caving), mastering the art of snowboarding or skiing, engaging in swimming, weightlifting, honing your skills at a cutting-edge fitness center, or indulging in a riveting game of racquetball at one of the esteemed indoor sports centers or schools you'll undoubtedly encounter during your visit. Furthermore, there are a multitude of high school and college sports teams in Idaho that captivate the unwavering attention of the individuals residing in this thriving region.

Idaho's reputation as a great place to be active has grown dramatically over the years, drawing more attention and attracting outdoor enthusiasts from all around the world. With its breathtaking landscapes and diverse climate zones, Idaho offers a plethora of opportunities for engaging in a wide range of outdoor sports and activities. From soaring mountain peaks to tranquil lakes and rivers, the state's natural beauty serves as the perfect playground for adventure seekers.

Idaho's four distinct seasons further enhance its appeal, providing a unique and dynamic backdrop for outdoor enthusiasts. Whether it's skiing down powdery slopes during the snowy winters, hiking through vibrant forests in the refreshing spring, enjoying watersports on crystal-clear lakes during the sunny summers, or exploring colorful trails amidst the breathtaking autumn foliage, Idaho caters to every outdoor passion throughout the year.

What sets Idaho apart is its exceptional diversity in climate zones, which is unparalleled compared to many other states. This allows for a wide variety of outdoor sports and activities that are exclusive to Idaho and just a handful of similar clement-type climate regions across the country. Whether you're a fan of skiing, mountain biking, fishing, whitewater rafting, rock climbing, or simply enjoying a peaceful picnic amidst nature's splendor, Idaho offers it all.

It's no wonder that Idaho has earned the well-deserved title of the Outdoor Sports Mecca of the United States. The state's abundant natural resources, coupled with its impeccable preservation efforts, create an environment that is both awe-inspiring and invigorating. Visitors flock to Idaho not just for its exceptional outdoor opportunities but also to experience the unique charm of its welcoming communities and immerse themselves in the captivating local culture.

In conclusion, Idaho's allure as a state to visit has surged alongside its reputation as an outdoor enthusiast's paradise. With a vibrant tapestry of landscapes, a multitude of climate zones, and an endless array of outdoor sports and activities, Idaho offers an extraordinary experience that leaves a lasting impression on all who venture here. Whether you seek thrilling adventures or peaceful moments of tranquility, Idaho is sure to exceed your expectations and provide memories that will last a lifetime.

30.1. Professional and Amateur Sports Teams

Racing The Snake River Raceway is a thrilling and adrenaline-pumping drag racing strip nestled in the stunning Caldwell area. Offering a heart-pounding experience like no other, this renowned racing haven boasts a myriad of exhilarating events that will leave race enthusiasts awestruck. From lightning-fast drag races to jaw-dropping feats of automotive engineering, there is something for everyone at the Snake River Raceway.

This adrenaline-fueled haven guarantees an unforgettable experience for both spectators and participants alike. Whether you're a seasoned racing aficionado or a curious newcomer, the Snake River Raceway caters to all. Feel the surge of power as the engines roar and the ground trembles beneath your feet. Embrace the electrifying atmosphere as you witness magnificent racing machines effortlessly conquer the tarmac, leaving streaks of blazing speed in their wake.

As you immerse yourself in this unparalleled racing extravaganza, marvel at the sheer dedication and passion of the talented drivers who push their high-performance vehicles to their limits. Their skill, precision, and unwavering determination weave a tapestry of awe-inspiring racing moments that will leave you breathless.

For those seeking an up-close and personal experience, the Snake River Raceway offers various opportunities to get involved. Whether you aspire to conquer the strip yourself or prefer to feel the rush of being a passenger during a heart-stopping ride-along, these adrenaline-fueled adventures are sure to satisfy your need for speed.

Prepare to be captivated by the sights and sounds of roaring engines, screeching tires, and the electrifying atmosphere that permeates every inch of the Snake River Raceway. Immerse yourself in this adrenaline-soaked world, where speed and precision reign supreme.

To learn more about this thrilling motorsports destination and plan your next pulse-pounding adventure, contact the Snake River Raceway today at (208) 455-4212. Get ready to rev your engines and unleash your inner speed demon at one of the most electrifying drag racing strips in the Caldwell area. Let the excitement begin!

Hockey The Idaho Steelheads, an East Coast Hockey League farm team of the Dallas Stars, call the Idaho Centre (16200 Idaho Centre Avenue, Nampa, Idaho) home. Situated in the heart of the Treasure Valley, this state-of-the-art facility offers a premier experience for both players and fans alike. Boasting spacious stands, modern amenities, and a lively atmosphere, the Idaho Centre is the ultimate destination for hockey enthusiasts.

Whether you're a die-hard fan or new to the sport, the Idaho Steelheads promise an exhilarating display of talent and fierce competition. From the thunderous roar of the crowd to the sound of blades carving through the ice, you'll be captivated by the energy that permeates the arena. Immerse yourself in the passion and excitement as the team battles their way towards victory.

The Idaho Centre is more than just a hockey rink; it's a community hub that fosters a sense of unity and pride among its spectators. Grab a bite to eat at one of the delicious concession stands, proudly displaying a variety of culinary delights. Indulge in a hot dog slathered with all your favorite toppings or savor a piping-hot slice of pizza. Quench your thirst with a refreshing beverage as you cheer on your favorite players.

For those seeking a truly immersive experience, VIP box seats offer unbeatable views along with exclusive perks. Pamper yourself with premium seating and access to a private lounge, where you can indulge in delectable treats and mingle with fellow hockey enthusiasts. Immerse yourself in the luxury of personalized service while never missing a single moment of the thrilling action on the ice.

Don't miss out on the opportunity to witness the Idaho Steelheads in action at the Idaho Centre. With a seating capacity that caters to thousands of fans, there is more than enough room for everyone to join in on the excitement. Mark your calendars and gather your friends and family for an unforgettable night of heart-pounding hockey.

To learn more about upcoming games, ticket availability, and special promotions, please contact the Idaho Steelheads at (208) 383-0080. Get ready to embrace the thrill of the game and create memories that will last a lifetime. Hurry, the action awaits!

Football Boise State University has hosted NCAA Division I Football Championships several times at Bronco Stadium, which has established itself as a renowned venue for thrilling gridiron battles. Sitting amidst the picturesque landscapes of Boise, Idaho, this remarkable stadium stands as a stage where the Boise State Broncos, a symbol of pride and determination, exemplify true sportsmanship and inspire countless fans. Spectators from all corners of the United States gather to witness the fierce competition between the Broncos and college teams hailing from diverse regions. The electrifying atmosphere charged with enthusiasm and anticipation permeates the air as the crowd unites in exuberant cheers and unwavering support for their beloved team. Broncos games are not merely sporting events, but rather captivating spectacles that showcase the power of dedication, teamwork, and the sheer joy of the game. Immerse yourself in the spirit of football excellence and be part of this unforgettable experience. For further inquiries and ticket information, kindly reach out to us at (208) 426-4737.

Boise, the capital and largest city of Idaho, has recently garnered significant attention in the sports world, as it has been granted the prestigious opportunity to host a brand new NBA franchise. This exciting development will pave the way for a thrilling basketball experience in Boise, reaching its pinnacle at the state-of-the-art Bank of America Centre.

Anticipation is mounting as the community eagerly awaits the inaugural season of this phenomenal NBA team, set to commence in the upcoming 2013-2014 season. Alongside this exciting news, the team is also preparing to unveil their distinct and compelling name, which will undoubtedly become a defining feature of their identity for seasons to come.

The vibrant city of Boise, known for its picturesque landscapes and welcoming atmosphere, is poised to become a basketball hub, attracting fans from every corner of the state and beyond. The Bank of America Centre, with its cutting-edge facilities and impeccable design, will undoubtedly provide the perfect stage for exhilarating basketball showdowns, as well as fostering a sense of unity and pride among its passionate supporters.

With a rich history of successful sports teams across various disciplines, Boise is ready to embrace this new venture, injecting a fresh energy into its already thriving sports scene. As the countdown to the inaugural season begins, excitement fills the air, and the entire community eagerly awaits the tip-off that will mark the beginning of a new era in Boise's sporting legacy.

Basketball The Idaho Stampede, an Independent League Association farm team for the Indiana Pacers, call the Bank of America Centre (260 S. Capitol Blvd.) home. If you're looking to catch an exciting game or support the team, you can easily find them at this iconic venue. The Bank of America Centre, located conveniently at 260 S. Capitol Blvd., is where all the thrilling basketball action takes place. With its state-of-the-art facilities and welcoming atmosphere, it's the ideal place to gather with friends, family, or fellow basketball enthusiasts to cheer on your favorite team. Make sure to mark your calendars and save the date for an unforgettable experience. To learn more about upcoming games, ticket availability, or any other inquiries, feel free to contact the Idaho Stampede at (208) 331-8497. Get ready to be part of the electrifying energy that fills the Bank of America Centre and witness the incredible skills and talents of the Idaho Stampede. Don't miss out on the excitement — grab your tickets today!

Baseball is a beloved sport that has captivated the hearts of millions around the world. In Boise, Idaho, the Boise Hawks proudly represent the Pioneer League as a farm team for the esteemed Colorado Rockies. Their home stadium, Memorial Stadium, which is located at 562 N. Broadway, serves as a hallowed ground where thrilling matches and unforgettable memories are made.

If you are seeking more information about the Boise Hawks or interested in attending one of their electrifying games, you can reach out to their knowledgeable team by dialing (208) 322-8316. They will be more than happy to provide you with any details or answer any questions you may have.

Baseball is not merely a game; it is a passion that unites communities and ignites a sense of camaraderie. With the Boise Hawks proudly representing their city, the spirit of baseball is alive and thriving in the heart of Idaho. Don't miss out on the chance to witness the exhilarating moments at Memorial Stadium as the Boise Hawks continue to make their mark in the Pioneer League.

CHAPTER-THIRTY ONE

31. Idaho's LGBTQ+ Friendly Spaces

In a recent survey conducted, it was found that a significant proportion of LGBTQ+ (lesbian, gay, bisexual, transgender, and queer/ing) individuals residing in Idaho, approximately 45.9%, reported facing discrimination within the state due to their sexual orientation. Furthermore, the study revealed that approximately 18.2% of LGBTQ+ individuals in Idaho experienced discrimination based on their gender expression. These distressing statistics highlight the persistent presence of discrimination within the state.

Despite these alarming figures, it is essential to acknowledge that numerous Idahoans and businesses actively promote LGBTQ+ inclusivity. The City of Boise, in particular, has emerged as a beacon of progress, consistently demonstrating its commitment to supporting the LGBTQ+ community. For several years now, the city has pioneered the provision of domestic partner benefits to its employees. Additionally, it has vigorously advocated for LGBTQ+ inclusivity within the Idaho Legislature. The unwavering support extended by the City of Boise is further reinforced by the presence of several openly LGBTQ+ city employees, including the first two openly gay City Council members and its first transgender police officer. Such inclusivity has been a defining characteristic of the city for decades, thereby fostering a welcoming and supportive environment for LGBTQ+ residents.

Furthermore, the establishment of an official tourism marketing arm for the State of Idaho has opened up new opportunities. This development has facilitated the application process for downtown Boise to acquire membership within the esteemed International Gay and Lesbian Travel Association (IGLTA). Consequently, LGBTQ+ individuals from all corners of the state can actively participate in pride events held in Boise on the third Saturday of June, as well as in Idaho Falls on the third Saturday of September. These events serve as key platforms for fostering unity, celebration, and pride within the LGBTQ+ community.

The progress made within Boise and the state of Idaho at large signifies a remarkable stride towards a more inclusive society. However, it is crucial to recognize that continued efforts are necessary to eradicate discrimination and create a safe and embracing environment for all LGBTQ+ individuals throughout the state. Through ongoing advocacy, education, and open dialogue, Idaho has the potential to become a model for LGBTQ+ inclusiveness and acceptance on a national scale.

31.1. Inclusive Bars and Community Centers

But bars may not be your type of place, and you would rather find something a bit more cultured and sophisticated. Many vibrant and diverse cities around the world boast a myriad of community centers that transcend mere entertainment and recreation—they are dedicated to nurturing a harmonious society for all. By taking the time to visit one or simply conducting a quick search online, you will uncover a treasure trove of knowledge not only about the rich and vibrant culture of the region but also about the essence and character of the place itself. Astute business owners actively engage with these platforms to express their concerns, acting as beacons of caution in highlighting establishments that may be best avoided. Their invaluable insights provide you with a comprehensive understanding of your potential destinations, ensuring that you make informed decisions about where to visit based on firsthand experiences shared among fellow community members.

When traveling to new destinations, whether it be for leisure or business, there will come a time where you find yourself seeking the comforts of a local bar. While it may seem tempting to gravitate towards the bars with the largest selection, it is crucial to understand that not all bars cater to everyone's needs. Some establishments only cater to specific groups, leaving others feeling alienated and unwelcome. Opting for such bars might hinder your ability to create lasting memories, regardless of whether you consume alcoholic beverages or not. Therefore, it is highly recommended to invest your time and effort in discovering a more inclusive bar, where the sole purpose is to create a delightful and memorable experience for every individual who walks through their doors. These establishments not only prioritize serving up a great time but also go the extra mile to ensure that visitors, like yourself, feel embraced and valued. In fact, the locals at these bars often exceed expectations, extending their hospitality by sharing insightful tips and recommendations to enhance your overall enjoyment of the city. By actively seeking out these inclusive havens, you can guarantee a genuinely happy and fulfilling time during your stay.

CHAPTER–THIRTY TWO

32. Idaho's Pet-Friendly Places

Highlight Night Ski or Snowshoe Dog Event at Gold Run Trails is an incredible evening adventure that enthralls both ski and snowshoe enthusiasts alike. This spectacular event takes place under the veil of night, as the trails are adorned with enchanting lights that cast a magical glow on the snowy landscape. As the moon peeks through the trees, participants are drawn into a world of snowy wonder as they embark on their thrilling journey.

One paramount rule that all dog owners must remember is that retractable leashes are strictly prohibited during this event. This safety measure ensures that both humans and their furry companions can navigate the trails with ease and without any potential entanglements. By adhering to this rule, everyone can focus solely on basking in the exhilarating experience that awaits them.

The adventure begins with Loop 1, an intriguing 2-mile trail that descends gracefully, mesmerizing participants with every step they take. Along this path, a delightful 150-foot change in elevation adds an element of excitement, amplifying the sense of adventure. The trail guides participants in a captivating counter-clockwise direction, offering breathtaking views of the awe-inspiring Rock Creek, especially when passing under the charismatic bridge. The charm of this scenic vista is truly unparalleled, leaving participants in awe of Mother Nature's masterpiece.

Loop 2, on the other hand, presents a longer and more profound journey into the heart of Gold Run Trails. Spanning over 5.5 miles, this descending trail leads intrepid adventurers in a mesmerizing clockwise direction that ultimately leads them to an inviting cabin. With each adventurous step taken, participants become more interconnected with the tranquility of the night and the captivating allure of the wintry landscape. Each turn, each gust of wind, and each snowflake that gently lands on their faces tell a unique story, igniting a sense of awe and wonder in the hearts of those who dare to embrace the unknown.

For those seeking an even lengthier and more extraordinary expedition, Loop 3 awaits to satisfy their thirst for challenge and triumph. Spanning an impressive 7.7 miles, this trail boasts a thrilling 350-foot change in elevation. The journey it presents is not for the faint of heart, as the challenging climbs that pepper the trail demand determination and resilience. While the climbs may be arduous, they reward participants with panoramic vistas that showcase the sublime scenery that surrounds Gold Run Trails. The feeling of accomplishment that washes over those who conquer this trail is immeasurable, as they stand atop the summit, looking down at the path they have conquered.

The challenging climbs may be routine for seasoned adventurers, yet they remain incredibly steep and require utmost dedication. It is within these moments of struggle that the true spirit of exploration emerges, as participants push beyond their limits and discover the immense strength that lies within. The rewards of conquering these steep climbs are unparalleled, as they serve as a reminder of the vastness of one's capabilities and the joys that await those who dare.

In conclusion, the Highlight Night Ski or Snowshoe Dog Event at Gold Run Trails offers a remarkable experience that transcends the ordinary. It is a celebration of winter's beauty and the indomitable spirit of exploration. Through breathtaking trails, enchanting lights, and a captivating sense of adventure, participants are transported to a world where the possibilities are limitless. So, gather your furry companions, adhere to the important leash rule, and embark on a journey that will leave you with memories to cherish for a lifetime.

Riverside Hot Springs Inn & Spa is a charming and timeless 1914 historic hotel nestled in the picturesque city of Lava Hot Springs. Offering a delightful escape from the hustle and bustle of city life, this enchanting establishment boasts an impressive collection of 18+ well-appointed rooms. Seeking to provide a truly charming experience for their guests, Riverside Hot Springs extends a warm welcome to small pets, ensuring that every member of the family can indulge in the tranquility and relaxation offered by this remarkable oasis.

Stepping into a world of timeless elegance, guests can revel in the absence of televisions in their immaculate rooms, fostering a sense of serenity and an opportunity to disconnect from the outside world. However, entertainment and bonding experiences are never far away, as the shared lobby becomes a haven for both humans and their canine companions. Engage in a friendly match of the exhilarating 'Horse Race' Bar Game, where excitement and laughter fill the air, creating unforgettable memories. For those seeking a creative adventure, embark on the captivating 'Selfie Scavenger Hunt,' exploring the hotel's charming nooks and crannies while capturing moments of joy with your beloved four-legged friend.

At Riverside Hot Springs, relaxation transcends the conventional expectations. Allow the tranquil ambiance and the soothing embrace of the spa to envelop your senses, as expert therapists pamper you with rejuvenating treatments that leave you feeling invigorated and refreshed. Indulge in a couples' massage, cherishing quality time with your loved one, or embark on a personal wellness journey, embracing the benefits of holistic therapies that nourish the mind, body, and soul.

As the sun sets over the breathtaking mountain landscape, immerse yourself in the soothing waters of the hot springs, embracing the therapeutic properties that have been cherished for generations. Discover the perfect balance between tranquility and adventure, as you explore the surrounding natural wonders, embark on exhilarating outdoor activities, or simply bask in the serenity of the hotel's delightful garden.

Whether you seek a romantic reprieve, a much-needed getaway, or a unique experience filled with laughter and joy, Riverside Hot Springs Inn & Spa offers an idyllic haven where treasured memories are waiting to be made. Come, indulge in the timeless charm and warm hospitality that awaits you at this remarkable historic gem in the heart of Lava Hot Springs.

Idaho Fish and Game Rental Cabins Lamping Homestead near Ketchum and Garden Creek near North Fork are 3 beautiful and cozy cabins and yurts that are exquisitely offered for rental to provide you with an unforgettable experience amidst nature's magnificent splendor. Rest assured that your furry friends are more than welcome to accompany you on this incredible journey, as dogs are cherished guests at these remarkable rental cabins and yurts, and the best part is, there's no additional cost for their accommodation.

We highly recommend choosing the perfect time to visit, as the off-season from late spring to fall seasons may prohibit any pets, serving as a precautionary measure to avoid any potential wildlife interference. However, worry not, for the tranquil and serene times commence during October and last until April, ensuring a truly idyllic and soul-soothing retreat. Immerse yourself in the breathtaking surroundings, embark on endless adventures, and create priceless memories in these remarkable havens of peace and tranquility.

Idaho City Hot Springs, nestled just north of the charming town of Idaho City, provides a picturesque retreat for all seeking rejuvenation and indulgence. Enveloped by the magnificent Springs at Idaho City, this enchanting haven boasts a collection of steamy hot springs pools that promise to immerse you in pure bliss. For a modest fee, immerse yourself in these soothing thermal waters and let your worries melt away.

Not only does Idaho City Hot Springs offer an oasis of relaxation, but it also takes care of your palate and entertainment needs. Indulge your senses in a culinary journey like no other, as the on-site dining options tantalize your taste buds with their delectable creations. From tantalizing appetizers to mouthwatering main courses, every bite is an experience to savor.

In addition to the gastronomic delights, Idaho City Hot Springs ensures that every moment spent here is filled with joy and merriment. As a newly introduced perk, owners can now delight in the company of their canine companions on dedicated days of the week. Watch your furry friends frolic and play in the designated areas, as their happiness mirrors your own.

Unwind, rejuvenate, and create unforgettable memories at Idaho City Hot Springs. Immerse yourself in luxurious tranquility, indulge in exquisite flavors, and revel in the company of loved ones – both two-legged and four-legged. Allow the Springs at Idaho City to be your sanctuary, where your longing for escape meets a world of ultimate relaxation and entertainment.

8th Street Market - Boise Dawg Day Afternoon can be felt in the air each August when the city's downtown merchants come together to celebrate and embrace the special bond between humans and their furry companions. This joyous occasion transforms the bustling streets into a vibrant and lively atmosphere, as the city's charming 8th Street is temporarily closed to traffic. The delightful melodies of music gracefully intermingle with the tantalizing aromas of delectable food, creating an irresistible ambiance that captivates both locals and visitors alike.

During this incredible event, you will find an abundance of captivating activities for both dogs and their devoted owners to enjoy. Countless booths, thoughtfully curated with an array of products and services, line the bustling thoroughfare. From high-end grooming salons that pamper your four-legged friends to specialized boutiques offering a delightful assortment of animal cuisine, there is something to cater to every canine need and desire. Exploring these exciting booths is an adventure in itself, as you discover an endless array of novel and distinctive items that are sure to pique your interest.

The entire 8th Street becomes a veritable haven for dog lovers, where passionate vendors showcase their unique creations and innovations. As you make your way through this dog-centric wonderland, you can't help but be enchanted by the infectious energy that permeates the air. Wagging tails, joyful barks, and friendly interactions between humans and canines create an atmosphere brimming with pure happiness. It is a celebration that highlights the extraordinary relationship between humans and their beloved furry companions.

Amidst the vibrant street market, you will also find a cornucopia of culinary delights that cater to both human and canine palates. Local food vendors proudly present a wide range of delectable treats, ensuring that no appetite goes unsatisfied. From mouthwatering gourmet hot dogs to scrumptious pup-friendly delicacies, there is an epicurean delight to suit every taste bud. As the tantalizing scents waft through the air, you can relish in the pleasure of savoring these delectable delights alongside your furry sidekick.

The enchantment of Boise Dawg Day Afternoon is not solely confined to the offerings of the street market. Beyond the vibrant stalls, a myriad of captivating events take place throughout the day, adding an extra layer of excitement to the festivities. From entertaining dog shows that showcase impressive tricks and talents to captivating seminars on pet care and well-being, there is an activity to engage every spectator. These events serve as a testament to the unwavering dedication and love that humans have for their faithful companions.

In summation, 8th Street Market - Boise Dawg Day Afternoon is a magnificent celebration that brings together the community in a harmonious fusion of wagging tails, delectable flavors, and joyful camaraderie. As the city's downtown merchants unite to honor the profound bond between humans and their furry friends, the streets of Boise are transformed into a captivating wonderland. It is a testament to the extraordinary connection that exists between us and our beloved dogs, and a beautiful reminder of the shared happiness we find in each other's company.

If you are anything like myself and take immense pleasure in the inimitable company of your beloved pets, who are undeniably significant and cherished members of your loving family, it is highly likely that you will deeply desire and yearn for their heartwarming companionship during your unforgettable journeys and adventures. However, this can pose certain unique challenges and obstacles to consider, particularly when your enchanting travels and expeditions take you to a diverse and fascinating array of captivating cities, beautiful counties, and even awe-inspiring states, each with its own allure and mystique. Nevertheless, fret not, for the exceptional state of Idaho, being predominantly renowned for its remarkable and extraordinary welcoming attitude towards our endearing and adored furry companions, indisputably proves to be an enchanting haven and paradise for devoted and passionate pet owners.

32.1. Pet-Friendly Accommodation and Parks

Your relentless and unwavering commitment, combined with your unwavering commitment to conducting meticulous research, can have a significant impact on guaranteeing that you and your cherished pets embark on an incredibly extraordinary and supremely gratifying excursion. Make it a priority to savor and luxuriate in each and every individual moment shared with your beloved furry companions, while conscientiously and diligently fulfilling your duty towards their welfare during the entire course of the upcoming expedition.

As long as you are well-prepared, you can still visit some parks with your pets in a responsible manner. Before you visit the park, please research the following:

1. Park regulations, which encompass rules and guidelines meant to maintain harmony and order within the park premises, preserving its natural beauty and offering everyone an enjoyable experience.

2. Pet exercise/travel supplies and accessories can prove to be incredibly beneficial when embarking on your park visit. Equipping yourself with these essentials ensures a trouble-free excursion, providing your beloved pets with the necessary items for exercise, comfort, and convenience.

3. Weather forecast – an essential aspect to consider before your park adventure. Staying informed about the forecasted weather conditions enables you to plan accordingly, taking into account suitable attire, protective gear, or any additional supplies necessary to ensure the utmost comfort and safety for both you and your furry companions.

4. Park visit risk and safety reminders – prioritize safety during your park visit, not only for your four-legged friends but for everyone involved. Heed the park's risk and safety reminders to ensure a seamless and secure experience. By adhering to these reminders, you can revel in the park's wonders, embracing its offerings while maintaining responsibility and compassion.

It is quite challenging, though not entirely impossible, to locate a park that warmly welcomes our beloved furry friends. It is of utmost importance that we abide by the park's rules and regulations in a strict manner, for the presence of pets on trails where they are explicitly forbidden remains the most prominent and pressing concern when it comes to the concept of pet-friendly parks.

Pet-friendly Parks

Having said that, if you really have to take your adorable and affectionate small, well-mannered pet with you, it is of utmost importance to meticulously plan your enchanting and memorable vacations. Ensure that every detail is carefully considered, from the breathtaking destinations to the exhilarating activities that will create everlasting memories for both you and your beloved furry companion. With your devoted pet by your side, embark on a journey filled with joy, laughter, and extraordinary adventures, knowing that you have prepared immaculately. Book accommodations that warmly welcome not only you but also your delightful pet, where the doors will be flung open with immense hospitality and genuine warmth. Create unforgettable moments as you explore new horizons together, cherishing the boundless love and undeniable connection that exists between you and your extraordinary pet.

Only a few Idaho accommodation providers are willing to accommodate your furry friends during your vacation. It is understandable that most luxury hotels are hesitant to do so due to the varying interpretations of what it means to be pet-friendly. The way you treat your pets as family members may not align with everyone else's perception. Additionally, it is a well-known fact that many pet owners do not fulfill their responsibility of cleaning up after their beloved companions when necessary. This can create challenges for hotels that allow pets on their premises. However, there are still establishments that warmly welcome pets and ensure a comfortable stay for both you and your furry companions.

Pet-friendly Accommodation

Bringing your beloved furry companions along on a memorable vacation can truly transform an already electrifying trip into an utterly extraordinary experience. However, embarking on this endeavor can sometimes prove to be quite challenging, as locating lodging or recreational areas that warmly welcome your pets with open arms may not always be a walk in the park. To alleviate any worries and ensure an unforgettable getaway for both you and your four-legged family members, here is but a mere glimpse of the myriad of pet-friendly accommodations and picturesque parks that eagerly await your arrival, eagerly pawing at the chance to cater to your every pet-related need and desire.

CHAPTER-THIRTY THREE

33. Idaho's Volunteer and Community Projects

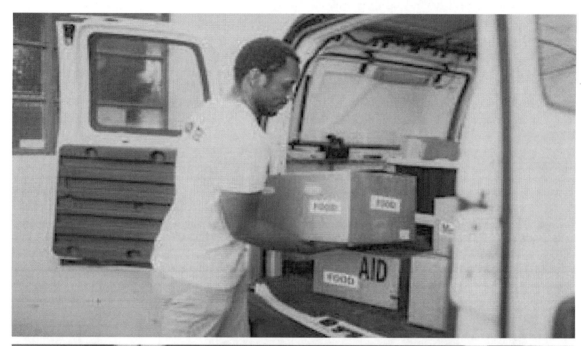

Some volunteer jobs, such as those associated with the Bitterroot National Forest, Idaho Fish and Game, Idaho Department of Parks and Recreation, the Bureau of Land Management, or the USDI National Park Service, are incredibly popular to the point where it might become necessary to make a reservation a full year in advance. For the majority of volunteer work, you won't find any specific job listings in agency files. To get involved in a project, tourists or travelers passing through Idaho should make it a point to stop by any government office, community program headquarters, or outdoor event to register their interest in contributing their efforts. Alongside this, while inquiring with the Idaho Division of Tourism, take the opportunity to learn about the various opportunities that might be available. However, it's important to note that insurance coverage is exclusive to Idaho volunteers and is only provided when the work is carried out under the official direction of a specific organization. Above all, we hope you have a safe, incredibly fulfulling, and immensely enjoyable stay in the beautiful state of Idaho, filled with countless memories and gratifying experiences that will last a lifetime.

Idaho, the beautiful state known for its breathtaking landscapes and vibrant communities, offers a myriad of captivating opportunities to embark on a fulfilling journey of volunteering and engaging in public services. The abundance of options available allows individuals to wholeheartedly contribute to their local communities while experiencing awe-inspiring travel escapades and embracing unique surroundings.

Moreover, Idaho generously provides numerous free camping sites, ensuring that volunteers receive tangible appreciation for their invaluable services. These campsites, equipped with comfortable tents and picturesque picnic areas, are a testament to Idaho's commitment to recognizing and uplifting the efforts of its selfless volunteers.

For those engrossed in ventures that require overnight volunteering to fulfill specific projects, Idaho goes above and beyond by facilitating prearranged free overnight camping. This thoughtful provision allows volunteers to seamlessly carry out their dedicated work while savoring the serenity and tranquility of Idaho's natural wonders. To ensure a hassle-free experience, it is advisable to check with the local agency involved regarding any required permits and essential tools necessary for the project.

In Idaho, every volunteering endeavor becomes an opportunity to foster personal growth, connect with like-minded individuals, and contribute to the overall betterment of society. Whether it is wielding tools to construct community projects or dedicating time towards public services, the vast array of opportunities in Idaho promises to leave an indelible mark on both the volunteers and the communities they serve.

33.1. Opportunities for Giving Back

Serve at a fish hatchery, restore habitats, or eradicate invasive plant species. Become an Idaho Conservation Corps Corpsmember for ages 18 to 25 years and contribute to the invaluable mission of preserving our natural environment. Join the Payette National Forest in wildland restoration, where your dedication will make a tangible difference in the preservation of this precious ecosystem. Help the Caribou-Targhee National Forest weed out the spotted knapweed and thistle that could potentially pose a threat to the native species and forage for the local wildlife, enabling the region's delicate balance to flourish. Perhaps you have the opportunity to lend your time and talents to the Teton Valley community and the U.S. Forest Service, continuing the vital work of restoring the Teton Pass Heritage Area, ensuring its cultural and ecological significance endures for generations to come. The opportunities to serve and make a lasting impact are truly boundless, and the rewards are immeasurable both for yourself and the world around you.

Given the vast array of natural resources available in the beautiful state of Idaho, there are countless and incredibly diverse opportunities to offer our services and make a positive impact on others. Within the expansive realm of Idaho's many national and state parks, an extraordinary range of possibilities awaits, allowing us to work side by side with a wide array of tourists hailing from every corner of the globe. With an astonishing expanse of over four million acres of public land at our disposal, the potential to serve as a vital force for good alongside esteemed organizations such as the U.S. Bureau of Land Management and the U.S. Forest Service becomes an inviting reality. In virtually every nook and cranny of this magnificent state, volunteer vacation opportunities flourish abundantly, beckoning us to partake in the benevolent act of giving back to our community. Regardless of whether one chooses to offer a few precious hours or embark on an entire vacation dedicated to this noble cause, the mere chance to contribute to the preservation and enhancement of Idaho's remarkable outdoors presents itself as a gateway to not only pursuing our individual passions but also leaving a lasting and tangible legacy that ensures the land is left in an even better condition than when we first graced its presence.

CHAPTER THIRTY-FOUR

34. Idaho's Wellness and Spa Retreats

34. BOISE, ZENESSE HEALTH, BEAUTY, AND WELLNESS SPA. As complete a pampering solution as the name implies, Boise's Zenesse offers an extensive range of full spa facilities, including state-of-the-art equipment and luxurious amenities. Additionally, Zenesse provides a wide variety of health and beauty services that cater to your specific needs, ensuring you receive the utmost care and attention. From the soothing and rejuvenating benefits of aromatherapy to the innovative N.A.E.T. services that promote overall well-being, Zenesse is committed to enhancing your personal wellness journey. Indulge in the therapeutic wonders of reflexology, a holistic treatment that aims to restore balance and harmony to your body and mind. With highly skilled and experienced professionals, Zenesse guarantees exceptional service and an unforgettable spa experience.

BOISE, GROVE HOTEL SPA. The magnificent 4500-sq-ft spa at The Grove Hotel, nestled in the heart of downtown Boise, is a true oasis of tranquility and serenity. Immerse yourself in a world of ultimate relaxation as you indulge in a wide variety of spa services that cater to your every need. From invigorating massages to revitalizing facial treatments, the Grove Hotel Spa offers a comprehensive menu of luxurious experiences that will leave you feeling refreshed and rejuvenated. But it doesn't stop there – the spa also provides full fitness services for those looking to maintain a healthy lifestyle. Dive into the crystal-clear waters of the indoor pool, unwind in the soothing whirlpool, or partake in a variety of invigorating exercise classes in the state-of-the-art exercise studio. The Grove Hotel Spa is your ultimate destination for well-being and self-care.

Center yourself in the vibrant Hyde Park, a bustling and lively commercial and cultural hub located in Boise's charming North End. This unique neighborhood is a true gem, offering a shady and walkable slice of historic Boise. Immerse yourself in the picturesque surroundings of friendly cottages, each with its own distinct character, and discover one-of-a-kind landmarks that serve as symbols of the neighborhood's rich heritage. Hyde Park is not just a place, but a community – a warm and welcoming haven filled with local businesses that treasure the beauty and history of Boise. Explore the charming shops, savor delectable cuisines in cozy restaurants, and experience the vibrant atmosphere of this remarkable neighborhood. Hyde Park is where Boise's past and present coexist harmoniously, inviting you to embrace its charm and create unforgettable memories.

It turns out that when you're constantly and perpetually surrounded by the breathtaking and awe-inspiring wonders of Mother Nature's gift, as us proud Idahoans are fortunate enough to be, you find yourself naturally and effortlessly drifting into a state of profound relaxation and rejuvenation. Idaho's heavenly and serene wellness and spa retreats breathe life into their idyllic and blissful surroundings, offering an exquisite array of opulent and indulgent spa treatments that utilize only the finest locally-sourced, organic products. These divine havens of well-being also provide integrated health services, meticulously crafted bodywork and massage that work harmoniously to melt away any lingering traces of stress and tension, and meticulously curated facilities that are expertly designed to soothe and nurture both the body and mind.

Whether nestled within the majestic embrace of the towering mountains or gently nestled along the tranquil shores of serene lakes, Idaho's wellness and spa retreats boast an astonishing variety of idyllic settings that cater to every individual's desires and preferences, ranging from intimate and boutique experiences to expansive and all-encompassing resorts that offer an extensive range of world-class amenities. Despite their diverse locations and distinctive atmospheres, the essence and underlying philosophy of these extraordinary oases of rejuvenation remains unwaveringly consistent - a commitment to providing an unparalleled and consistently invigorating experience for each and every guest.

Make sure to keep a watchful eye and an eager anticipation for the awe-inspiring treatments and enchanting visits that incorporate the essence of Idaho through the utilization of delectable honey, tantalizing huckleberries, aromatic herbs, and an array of other delightful local delicacies. These tantalizing additions serve to further elevate and enrich the entire wellness and spa experience, imbuing it with a uniquely Idahoan charm that effortlessly transports you to a world overflowing with opulence, tranquility, and holistic nourishment for the senses.

34.1. Relaxation and Healing Centers

The centerpiece of the Lower Stanley neighborhood is the Mountain Village Resort, an exquisite establishment that boasts a plethora of luxurious amenities for guests to indulge in. Among these offerings, the resort features a mesmerizing mineral spring-fed pool, providing a tranquil oasis for individuals to unwind and rejuvenate their senses. Additionally, the resort is equipped with a state-of-the-art spa, a haven of relaxation that offers an array of treatments and services designed to melt away stress and promote overall well-being. Furthermore, for those seeking an invigorating workout, the resort provides a top-notch fitness center boasting breathtaking panoramic views of the awe-inspiring rugged Sawtooth Mountain Range, making each exercise session an unforgettable experience.

When it comes to pools and health and wellness experiences, Idaho has no shortage of exceptional options. The vibrant city of Boise beckons with its remarkable selection of rejuvenating swimming pools and wellness centers, catering to the needs and desires of every individual seeking solace and tranquility. The charming community of Meridian, nestled amidst the picturesque landscapes of rural Idaho, also presents an array of delightful pools and wellness establishments, offering a serene escape from the stresses of everyday life. Furthermore, the enchanting city of Lewiston, known for its idyllic surroundings, boasts a variety of outstanding venues where visitors can immerse themselves in ultimate relaxation, discovering a sense of tranquility unique to this captivating region.

While rural retreats in Idaho are renowned for their ability to provide a serene and peaceful atmosphere, urban havens such as Boise's esteemed Body Calm have captured the hearts and minds of our esteemed readers. Highly recommended for those in search of a truly unforgettable experience, Body Calm offers a sanctuary of tranquility amidst the bustling city. Step into a world of serenity and allow yourself to be pampered by skilled professionals who specialize in delivering the best massages, facials, body wraps, and various other heavenly treatments. With each visit, you will embark on a journey of ultimate relaxation, leaving all worries and stresses behind.

For a truly divine wellness experience, Snake River Zen Spa and Salon at the renowned Yoshioe Grand Hotel in Lewiston is an absolute must-visit. A world-class establishment, this exquisite spa and salon offer an extensive range of unparalleled treatments and services, meticulously designed to cater to the unique needs and desires of every individual. Immerse yourself in the lap of luxury as you indulge in a sensational massage, allowing your cares to drift away. Experience the rejuvenating effects of a revitalizing facial, leaving your skin glowing and refreshed. Envelop yourself in the soothing warmth of a body wrap, embracing a feeling of utter serenity. Finally, enjoy a polished treatment that will leave you feeling truly pampered and rejuvenated, ensuring you depart the salon feeling like royalty.

Discover the true essence of relaxation and revitalization in the captivating landscapes of rural Idaho. Whether you choose to embark on a blissful escape to the Mountain Village Resort in Lower Stanley or explore the countless other idyllic destinations in this remarkable region, rest assured that unforgettable wellness experiences await. Rejuvenate your mind, body, and soul as you immerse yourself in the serene ambiance of pools, spas, and wellness centers that have earned a place in the hearts of locals and visitors alike. Escape from the demands of everyday life and allow yourself the luxury of embracing tranquility in the enchanting embrace of Idaho's remarkable wellness establishments.

Old-fashioned mountain hot springs make for incredibly relaxing centers, and a multitude of spas have taken it to the next level by incorporating cutting-edge 21st-century treatments that cater to your unique style and needs. The prices for a wide range of offerings such as invigorating yoga sessions, indulgent massages, and therapeutic mineral soaks vary by facility, ensuring that there is something for everyone. However, what remains constant is the enchanting backdrop of breathtaking natural beauty that surrounds these remarkable havens of tranquility.

When it comes to group-friendly hot springs and pools, Burgdorf Hot Springs and Gold Fork Hot Springs stand out as exceptional choices. At Gold Fork Hot Springs, in particular, both of its outdoor pools boast sandy bottoms, creating an experience akin to lounging on a pristine beach while being enveloped in the warmth of the mineral-rich water. Additionally, these pools are not only visually stunning but also offer the perfect opportunity to bond with your loved ones or make new friends in a serene and inviting atmosphere.

But it doesn't end there. The allure of hot springs extends to numerous other locations as well. Garden Valley, Lowman, and McCall, for instance, possess an abundance of both natural and commercially developed hot springs. These highly sought-after destinations offer a range of amenities such as clean and inviting concrete pools, well-maintained picnic areas for enjoying delicious meals amidst nature's wonders, and convenient RV parking facilities for a seamless and enjoyable experience.

The expansion of hot springs and spas in these regions allows for a myriad of experiences catered to individual preferences, all while basking in the unparalleled beauty of the surrounding landscapes. Whether you are seeking solitude, rejuvenation, or social connections, these awe-inspiring hot springs guarantee an unforgettable and truly transformative experience. So, immerse yourself in the enchanting waters, let the soothing touch of expert therapists melt away your cares, and find solace in the harmonious symphony of nature and relaxation.

CHAPTER-THIRTY FIVE

35. Idaho's Educational and Learning Opportunities

Educational and learning opportunities are abundantly provided by a myriad of esteemed establishments in Idaho. These include illustrious museums, state-of-the-art visitor centers, resourceful libraries, captivating art galleries, enlightening interpretive sites, remarkable natural landscapes for outdoor exploration and recreation, as well as cutting-edge science centers. Moreover, Idaho boasts university-sponsored statewide cooperative Extension Service programs that showcase the state's commitment to academic excellence.

In addition to these remarkable resources, Idaho's parks offer exceptional learning experiences for all. Snowhaven, a truly unique state-owned and operated winter sports park nestled in the picturesque Grangeville, allows individuals to delve into the thrilling world of snow sports. Meanwhile, Cataldo Mission at Cataldo stands as a testament to Idaho's rich history, providing an educational journey into the state's fascinating past. And not to be forgotten, Centennial Trail State Park, located near the enchanting Coeur d'Alene, and Lucky Peak State Recreation Park, near the vibrant city of Boise, beckon visitors with their awe-inspiring landscapes and countless opportunities for adventure and learning.

Continuing on this educational odyssey, Idaho's impressive array of sites dedicated to promoting the state's cherished heritage play a crucial role in nurturing values-based education. From wildlife refuges to well-equipped environmental learning centers, from breathtaking public lands and waters to meticulously preserved historic sites, Idaho ensures that its citizens and visitors have access to a wealth of educational and enlightening experiences. The interpretive exhibits housed within national parks, U.S. Forest Service offices, and Idaho Department of Commerce and Labor Jobs Connection career center sites serve as invaluable educational resources, providing a deeper understanding of various subjects.

The learning opportunities in Idaho are truly comprehensive, catering to a wide range of interests and disciplines. Students and enthusiasts can immerse themselves in the fascinating realms of earth and physical sciences, delve into the realms of technology and philosophy, explore the intricacies of communications, gain insights into the world of literature and language arts, advance their mathematical skills, and even explore vocational choices. The social sciences, including sociology, anthropology, and psychology, are also well-represented, allowing individuals to deepen their understanding of society and human behavior. Additionally, Idaho takes great pride in offering extensive education on the state's history and government, fostering an informed and engaged citizenry. Finally, the fine arts and music flourish within this vibrant state, allowing individuals to express themselves creatively and discover the pure beauty of artistic expression.

Above all, Idaho stands as an exemplar of fiscal solvency and responsible budgeting. Its long-standing tradition of prudent financial management is unparalleled, setting a remarkable standard for other states to follow. By embodying these principles, Idaho serves as a shining beacon of economic stability and serves as an inspiration to all who seek to achieve lasting financial prosperity and success.

Genuine discovery invites you to stretch your mind and stir your imagination, embarking on a magnificent journey of knowledge that transcends boundaries. It educates the heart and head, unveiling a treasure trove of profound wisdom and boundless creativity. Idaho's educational offerings provide an extraordinary array of unique opportunities for curious travelers like yourself, eager to embark on a transformative quest to expand your comfort zone, broaden horizons, and immerse in the wonders of enlightenment.

In the remarkable landscapes of Idaho, learning becomes an exhilarating adventure in itself, akin to the breathtaking thrill of leaping off a towering bridge, embracing the exhilarating sensation of weightlessness as you soar through the air, your spirit unfettered and liberated. It's like savoring a blissful day at a luxurious spa, where each moment is a gentle caress of rejuvenation and serenity, nurturing both body and soul.

Picture yourself paddling along the majestic Middle Fork of the Salmon River, a magnificent symphony of nature's grandeur that orchestrates harmony within your being. Every stroke of your paddle resonates with the rhythm of the river, guiding you towards a deeper understanding of the world and your place within it. Or perhaps, imagine embarking on a trail ride on a crisp autumn day, where the gentle rustling of leaves beneath your horse's hooves becomes a melodic narrative, whispering tales of ancient wisdom and forging an unbreakable bond between man and nature.

The hospitable and friendly nature of Idahoans embodies a spirit of warmth and kinship, enveloping you in a sense of belonging as you traverse the magnificent landscapes that span the entire island. Engaging in open conversations with the locals, sharing stories and laughter over hearty meals, you become part of a vibrant tapestry of camaraderie that unites seekers of knowledge from all walks of life.

In Idaho, every corner is imbued with the essence of enlightenment, inviting you to delve into the deepest recesses of your being and emerge with newfound clarity and valuable insights. So let your curiosity guide you, as you embark on a transformative journey through Idaho's educational offerings, where the wonders of discovery await at every turn.

35.1. Workshops and Classes

Terry Lee Workshops - Terry Lee, a highly accomplished and skilled Pottery Artist, has developed an exceptional and extraordinary program dedicated to providing unparalleled accommodations and facilitation for individuals with a profound interest in acquiring the remarkable artistry of pottery. The classes, meticulously crafted and held in Terry Lee's welcoming home/studio, offer a transformative experience like no other. With an incredibly limited number of spots available, students can partake in two awe-inspiring classes per week, cherishing every moment of their artistic journey. These classes are designed in convenient

4-8-week sessions, allowing learners to fully immerse themselves in the captivating world of pottery. Moreover, the classes commence right at the inception of each month, ensuring a comprehensive and seamless learning experience for all attendees.

To make this entire artistic odyssey even more extraordinary, Terry Lee's all-inclusive package has incorporated exceptional accommodations for all participants. By tapping into this exceptional package, class members are granted unrestricted access to an array of outstanding facilities, empowering them to create and learn clay molding at their own pace, with absolute freedom. Additionally, within these awe-inspiring 4 to 5-day sessions, students are presented with an incredible opportunity to extend their stay and transform it into a two-week-long vacation, indulging in relaxation and savoring the artistic atmosphere to their heart's content. Not only are accommodations catered solely for students, but provisions have also been thoughtfully made for non-student companions who wish to savor a captivating and unforgettable vacation alongside their artistic counterparts.

For those captivated by the prospect of enrolling in these extraordinary pottery classes or partaking in the exhilarating studio sale days, Terry kindly requests that you express your interest without hesitation. Classes are meticulously scheduled to commence in the splendid and vibrant month of September, with future months to be determined based on meticulous and well-thought-out scheduling. Moreover, to provide aspiring individuals with an opportunity to participate in this mesmerizing journey, the studio will open its doors to the public during the magnificent months of January, April, July, and November. These instances serve as the perfect occasion for individuals to eagerly sign up for upcoming classes or acquire breathtaking pieces during the studio sale days, further cementing Terry Lee's dedication to the vibrant artistic community.

Sawtooth Mountain Guides, Inc. - Wilderness Adventure Learning Resorts. Based in Stanley, Idaho, the company specializes in backcountry travel by conducting comprehensive instructional mountaineering, rock-climbing, and ice-climbing programs in the breathtaking Sawtooth Mountains that encircle the greater Sawtooth area. Offering a diverse array of thrilling programs, Sawtooth Mountain Guides extends its expertise throughout Central Idaho, catering to adventure enthusiasts who yearn to explore the untamed wilderness. In addition, their renowned U.S. East, U.S. West, and Canadian winter climbing programs are available, providing an opportunity for daring climbers to conquer magnificent icy heights. Each expedition with Sawtooth Mountain Guides promises an unforgettable journey through the most awe-inspiring and picturesque wilderness areas that North America has to offer.

River Moments - High Adventure Outdoor Photography - Experience the breathtaking beauty of untouched and expansive wilderness landscapes, where the serenity of flowing rivers creates a mesmerizing symphony with nature's untouched beauty. Embrace the unparalleled thrill of encountering dynamic wildlife in its most glorious form, as you capture their majestic essence through the lens of your camera. Immerse yourself in the camaraderie of like-minded individuals who share your passion for outdoor photography, as you embark on exhilarating group workshops and seminars that will expand your knowledge and skills. Let the wilderness adventures unfold before your eyes, as you traverse uncharted territories and unveil hidden treasures that only the brave dare to seek. Find solace in the peaceful ripples of mountain lake kayaks, transporting you to a world where tranquility and adventure harmoniously coexist. As the sun sets, gather around the enchanting campfire program, where stories are shared, laughter fills the air, and everlasting memories are forged. With utmost dedication, meticulously document each photography site, ensuring a continuous and comprehensive archival of your visual journey through the wilderness. Embark on the ultimate escapade where nature's spectacle, indomitable spirit, and the artistry of photography entwine to create countless moments of pure enchantment.

Betsy Jenson's Workshops and Retreats - Women's Art and Craft Workshops and Retreats focused on various creative endeavors to enhance your skills and ignite your passion for artistic expression. Immerse yourself in an array of captivating topics that encompass the world of art and craft, such as the art of scrapbooking, the intricate craftsmanship of jewelry making, the mesmerizing techniques of watercolor painting, the captivating world of decorative painting, and the enchanting world of creating delightful greeting cards, among others.

Our Retreats are carefully curated to provide a serene and inspiring environment for your artistic journey, nestled amidst the breathtaking landscapes of the scenic mountain town of Idaho City. Experience the tranquility and rejuvenation as you explore your creative side, surrounded by nature's essence in its purest form. The Platt Cabin, along with other splendid locations, offers a haven for your artistic pursuits, away from the hustle and bustle of everyday life.

Escape to our Women's Art and Craft Workshops and Retreats, where you can indulge your creativity, connect with like-minded individuals, and embrace the joy of crafting and creating. Unleash your artistic potential, learn new techniques, and discover a world brimming with endless possibilities. Betsy Jenson's Retreats and Workshops are a gateway to self-discovery, personal growth, and the sheer pleasure of immersing yourself in the captivating world of art and craft. Join us and embark on a transformative journey that will leave you inspired, enriched, and with treasured memories to cherish for a lifetime.

Artist Workshop - Stained Glass, Mosaics, Fused Glass, Beading, Photography, Portable Saw Mill, Woodworking. Tour of Elk Run Facility.

Discover your creative passion at the illustrious Artist Workshop, where you can immerse yourself in a multitude of captivating artistic endeavors. Unleash your imagination and ignite your artistic spirit as you explore the enchanting realms of Stained Glass, Mosaics, Fused Glass, Beading, Photography, Portable Saw Mill, and Woodworking. Delve into the intricate world of Stained Glass and witness the awe-inspiring beauty that emerges through the harmonious fusion of vibrant colors and delicate designs. Embark on an adventurous journey into the captivating realm of Mosaics and revel in the power of assembling countless tiny fragments to form breathtaking masterpieces. Experience the mesmerizing artistry of Fused Glass and witness firsthand how heat transforms raw glass into exquisite creations that radiate with captivating allure. Dive into the captivating domain of Beading and unravel the secrets of manipulating tiny beads to craft intricate jewelry and decorative pieces that will leave you in awe. Unleash your inner shutterbug as you delve into the enthralling world of Photography, where you'll learn to capture the essence of life through the lens of your camera, immortalizing moments that will last a lifetime. Immerse yourself in the world of Woodworking and discover the transformative power of timber as you create stunning, handcrafted pieces that showcase the beauty found within the veins of each wooden masterpiece. And if that weren't enough, embark on a fascinating Tour of Elk Run Facility, where you'll gain exclusive behind-the-scenes access and witness the magic unfold as skilled artisans bring their visions to life. Join us at the Artist Workshop and let your creativity soar to new heights as you explore a multitude of artistic disciplines that will awaken your senses, invigorate your soul, and leave you inspired beyond measure.

Artist Mineral and Art Guild Gallery - Located in the historic Idaho First National Bank building, the Artist Mineral and Art Guild Gallery serves as a captivating space that exudes creativity and admiration for the arts. Within this delightful gallery, visitors are treated to a magnificent display of artworks by talented local and regional artists, each piece possessing its own unique charm.

As you step through the gallery's entrance, you are immediately greeted by the vibrant colors and breathtaking scenes that adorn the walls. The gallery proudly showcases a wide array of artistic mediums, ensuring that every visitor finds something that sparks their interest. From mesmerizing watercolor paintings that capture the essence of nature, to richly textured oil masterpieces that evoke strong emotions, there is something to suit every artistic preference.

Immerse yourself in the world of pastel art, where delicate strokes create soft and dreamy landscapes. Marvel at the intricate glasswork, meticulously crafted with precision and transformed into awe-inspiring sculptures that play with the light. Feel the raw energy emanating from the metal and wood installations, each piece embodying strength and innovation. Lose yourself in the stories woven into the delicate paper art, showcasing the artist's meticulous attention to detail.

For those seeking a touch of tradition, the gallery proudly presents a collection of exquisite pottery and basketry. Admire the skill and craftsmanship that goes into creating each piece, marveling at the flawless forms and intricate designs. Witness the transformative power of raku, as the glaze crackles and smokey color patterns emerge, resulting in breathtaking ceramic creations that captivate the eye.

The gallery's commitment to showcasing artists extends even further with its collection of bronze sculptures, each reflecting the incredible talent and dedication of the artist. As you explore the gallery, don't forget to admire the limited edition prints of Smoky Mountain landscapes, capturing the beauty and majesty of this enchanting natural wonder.

With its diverse range of artistic mediums and a myriad of talented artists, the Artist Mineral and Art Guild Gallery is a treasure trove for art enthusiasts and appreciators alike. As you navigate its halls and take in the exceptional works on display, prepare to be moved, inspired, and delighted by the boundless creativity that emanates from every corner.

Workshops and classes are offered in a wide variety of fascinating areas of interest, ensuring an enriching experience for individuals seeking to enhance their creative skills and delve into new artistic pursuits. These captivating disciplines encompass the mesmerizing realms of stained glass, mosaics, scrapbooking, photography, quilting, jewelry creation, watercolor painting, baskets, flower arranging, the age-old art of blacksmithing, ceramic pottery, calligraphy, and a plethora of other captivating subjects that ignite the passion for art and creativity. Idaho, known for its thriving artistic community, boasts an array of acclaimed and accomplished artists who are brimming with enthusiasm about imparting their boundless wisdom and unrivaled expertise through unparalleled specialized two to five-day classes. Participants can expect to immerse themselves in an atmosphere of creative inspiration, foster connections with like-minded individuals, and discover new artistic techniques and approaches that will expand their horizons. These workshops and classes offer a unique opportunity for individuals of all skill levels to explore the depths of their artistic potential, providing a platform for personal growth, self-expression, and the cultivation of a lifelong appreciation for the arts. Join us in this artistic journey and unlock your creative genius as you embark on an unforgettable experience of artistic exploration and discovery.

CHAPTER THIRTY-SIX

36. Idaho's Religious and Spiritual Sites

With the coming of stability, religion emerged and grew in significance. A majority of the early settlers hailed from Mormon backgrounds, and their chapels and churches flourished exponentially. While the headquarters may have resided in Utah, the real work was being done in the vast expanses of Idaho. The efforts of the Episcopal missionary, Bishop Daniel Sylvester, were met with considerable success as he established parishes throughout the far reaches of Southern Idaho. In addition to this, Brune's Hot Springs became a haven for a group known as the Tasters, who had migrated from Chicago and created a picturesque community named Democracy. Christian Science served as the accepted religion in this idyllic colony. Adjacent to Democracy, a renowned church camp called The Green Cathedral House stood as a testament to faith and spirituality. An intriguing piece of history reveals that Mr. and Mrs. Varies purchased the property, which would later become their cherished church, for the remarkable price of $50.50. They became frequent attendees of Green's church and their dedication remains evident even today. Remarkably, the shaded lanes leading to the church are still accessible to cars for a nominal fee of $1.50, while human visitors are welcome to stay for an entire week, completely free of charge. Moving northwest from there, the Dixon area and surrounding locations became home to settlers who were members of the Church of the Brethren, popularly known as "Tunkers" or "Dunkurar." Their presence added to the rich religious tapestry of the region.

The links between Idaho and religion are sometimes a bit elusive, but they are definitely present. With such a minuscule population at the mid-point of the nineteenth century, very few religious services were held. However, amidst this spiritual scarcity, emerged a remarkable figure, Father Mesplie, a devout and vivacious Catholic priest. His reputation stemmed from his remarkable ability to endure arduous travels across vast distances in Idaho, tirelessly spreading the holy word of God to the early inhabitants who might be in need of spiritual guidance. Father Mesplie's unwavering dedication and unwavering commitment to his divine mission truly set him apart.

In addition to Father Mesplie, other religious leaders also left a lasting impact on Idaho's religious landscape. Rabbis Greenberg and Hochman were among the pioneers who relocated to southern Idaho for a period of time, where they wholeheartedly served the Jewish community. Their presence and devotion provided much-needed solace and support to the Jewish individuals residing in the region.

Another itinerant missionary, Rabbi Alexander M. Asher, played a crucial role in the establishment of several congregations in Idaho. With resolute determination and deep-rooted faith, Rabbi Asher tirelessly embarked on his evangelical journey, spreading the teachings of Jewish orthodoxy throughout various communities. During his travels, he visited Thatcher in 1917, Sugar City in 1918, and returned to Thatcher once more in 1922. These visits not only brought spiritual enlightenment but also paved the way for the formation of congregations that could adhere to the sacred principles and customs of Jewish orthodoxy.

Through the devotion and tireless efforts of these religious leaders, Idaho gradually developed a stronger religious foundation, nurturing the faith of its inhabitants and providing them with the spiritual nourishment they yearned for. Their unwavering commitment to their respective religious communities allowed Idahoans to seek solace, find meaning, and forge deeper connections with their faith during times of both joy and hardship.

36.1. Churches and Meditation Centers

Caldwell – Christian Science Society, 314 Blaine Friendship Community Church, 989 E. 7th Street Heart Springs Ecumenical Center, 838 Dickman Road College of Idaho Gershman Chapel, 2112 Cleveland Blvd. Murdoch Page house – Learning Resource Center Campus Chapel, 2112 Cleveland College of Idaho Filer – Full Gospel Lighthouse, 333 E. Chukar Hills Dr. Grand View – Assembly of God, 404 Three Rivers Lane; Bruneau Community Church, 203 S. Date; Joy Lutheran Church; United Church of Christ Homedale – Assembly of God, 10 Davis Ave. Jordan Valley – Christian Church, 60 N. Church St. Kuna – Christmas Church of Kuna, Friend's of Peace Church, 536 W. 4th; Kuna United Methodist Church, 260 W. 4th; Unity Church of Boise, 3986 W. Sims Marsing – Apostolic Afternoon Church Middleton – Grace N Faith Church, Middleton Church of the Nazarene, McCain Church of God, Middleton United

Methodist, Mejavic Spanish United Methodist, Duff's Evangelical Methodist, Lizard Butte Baptist Church Mtn. Home – Our Lady of Good Counsel, 459 NW Quincy St.; Elmore Baptist Church, Whites Residential Community Mtn. Home A. F. B. – Mountain Home Christian Center, 1250 S. Goodfellow Street, Chapel One Alconbury St Trees For Global Cooling Murphy Silver City Community Presbyterian Church, 904 Homedale Highway Nampa – The Lighthouse, Seventh-day Adventist Hospital, 159 E. Hawaii; Nampa Baptist Temple, 476 W. Karcher; Caldwell Seventh-day Adventist Church, 629 Edgewood, Salvation Army Church & Family Services, 16 1st St. New Plymouth – Friends of Peace, 303 E. Plymouth; St. Johns Catholic Church, 315 S. Mill Rd. Notus – Peace and Bread Church, 11 South 4th Parma – Church of God of Prophercy, 109 N. 6th; Church of Jesus Christ of Latter-day Saints, 303 E. Rose St.; Faith Assembly of God Church, Triangle Park; First Baptist Church Of Parma, 203 Wilkins Ave.; Church of the Nazarene, 219 N. 6th; St. Mary's Catholic Church, 611 W. Edwards Ave.; The Church of Priscilla Star – Nampa Alliance S. of G. Church, Unity S of G., 1811 E. Aire Park Dr. Unitarian Church, 16th and 6th Wilder – Lusitano Portuguese Fox Lane – Baptist. S. of G., Friends of Peace Church, Lusitano Sap Ropers, U. M; Wilder United Methodist Church, First Seattle Baptist Church of Wilder

CHAPTER THIRTY-SEVEN

37. Idaho's Accessibility and Inclusivity

Idaho is gradually becoming more accessible to people from all walks of life, regardless of their abilities. Although there is still progress to be made in terms of inclusivity and accessibility, a dedicated group of individuals is tirelessly working towards achieving this goal. Multiple cities, towns, businesses, and organizations are collaborating strenuously to ensure that Idaho caters to the needs of every individual, enabling them to visit, participate in events, and fully indulge in all that Idaho has to offer.

As an individual without personal experience regarding accessibility matters, I would defer to the numerous existing organizations and resources that delve into the diverse wonders of Idaho. These entities possess comprehensive knowledge about the state's accessibility, simultaneously outlining the many avenues through which individuals can explore Idaho's magnificence. Therefore, it's crucial to emphasize the importance of these resources in providing a bridge to those seeking to explore Idaho's breathtaking landscapes and vibrant communities.

To further enhance your experience and maximize accessibility during your visit, I would like to provide you with a broad compilation of some invaluable resources detailing the accessibility and inclusivity of Idaho. By contacting the local visitor center at your planned destination, you can acquire the most up-to-date and meticulously crafted information. The professionals at these visitor centers are well-versed in the diverse needs and requirements of individuals from all abilities, ensuring that your visit to Idaho is as seamless and fulfilling as possible.

Moreover, this step will grant you the opportunity to engage in a fruitful discussion about any concerns or queries you may have. Whether you have questions about accessible accommodations, transportation options, or specific attractions and events, the knowledgeable staff at the visitor centers will be more than happy to provide you with detailed information and personalized recommendations. Their expertise and dedication to accessibility will guarantee that you feel supported and empowered throughout your time in Idaho.

In addition to the local visitor centers, online resources are also available to assist you in planning your accessible journey through Idaho. These websites offer a wealth of information, including accessible hiking trails, wheelchair-friendly attractions, and inclusive festivals and activities. With just a few clicks, you can access a comprehensive guide to Idaho's accessible offerings, making it easier than ever to navigate the state's wonders.

By utilizing these resources and reaching out to local visitor centers, you can ensure that your visit to Idaho is not only enjoyable but also tailored to your specific accessibility needs. Idaho's commitment to inclusivity is evident in the collective efforts of its cities, towns, businesses, and organizations, all working tirelessly to create a welcoming environment for every individual. So whether you're seeking adventure in the majestic mountains, immersing yourself in the rich history and culture, or simply enjoying the warm hospitality of Idaho's communities, rest assured that accessibility awaits you at every turn.

37.1. Resources for Travelers with Disabilities

Idaho has a wide range of activities and offerings to cater to the diverse needs of every type of traveler. With a special focus on travelers with disabilities, the state has implemented numerous adaptations and accommodations to ensure inclusivity and accessibility.

To facilitate ease of communication, Idaho has incorporated Braille listings in the phonebook, allowing individuals with visual impairments to easily access important contact information. Furthermore, service clubs are actively involved in disseminating newsletters that highlight special events and activities specifically tailored for travelers with disabilities. These newsletters serve as a valuable resource, providing individuals with the most up-to-date information on inclusive events and programs.

Committing to the goal of enabling all members of the community to stay engaged and active, Idaho offers specialized transit programs. These programs allow individuals with disabilities to participate in the various activities and events taking place in their communities. With the help of these programs, travelers can maintain an active lifestyle and feel connected to their surroundings.

For a comprehensive list of the organizations and groups that provide these vital services, individuals can refer to the Idaho Travel Guide and the Area Resource File. These resources serve as comprehensive directories, ensuring that travelers with disabilities have access to all the necessary information they may require. The Idaho Department of Commerce is the primary source for obtaining copies of the Idaho Travel Guide, and interested parties can reach out to them for further information.

To gain a deeper understanding of the services available and the individuals who can benefit from them, it is recommended to contact the Idaho Transportation Department, Division of Public Transportation. They possess a wealth of knowledge and can provide valuable insights into the services offered and how they can cater to the specific needs of travelers with disabilities.

In conclusion, Idaho is fully committed to providing an inclusive and accessible environment for all travelers. With a wide range of adaptations and services in place, individuals with disabilities can confidently explore the state, participate in events, and remain active members of their communities.

CHAPTER THIRTY-EIGHT

38. Idaho's Emergency Contacts

Securities Division, Division of Finance: Reach out to the Idaho Securities Bureau by dialing 1-888-346-3378, which is their dedicated phone line, or alternatively, you can visit their official website. At the Idaho Securities Bureau website, you will have access to a plethora of valuable resources such as comprehensive information about securities, the ability to file complaints swiftly and effortlessly, and the opportunity to delve into detailed profiles of individuals, firms, or investments that pique your interest. We encourage you to leverage these services to make informed decisions and ensure the utmost safety and security in your financial endeavors.

Boating Education Course, Directed Inquiries: 1-800-253-1157 for scheduled classes WATER; *728 to report a complaint or non-emergency incident on the water; *77 on Call Box for information on Department of Parks and Recreation Water Safety. In addition to the law, anyone 21 or under must complete an approved Boating Education course and carry a Boating Safety Education Card when operating a motorboat, including personal watercraft. Email: boatedu@parksandrecreation.idaho.gov.

For more information about the Boating Education Course, including class schedules and inquiries, please contact us at 1-800-253-1157. Our dedicated team is ready to assist you and provide you with the necessary details for enrollment. Additionally, if you come across any complaint or non-emergency incident on the water, you can conveniently report it by dialing *728. Our reliable hotline guarantees that your concerns will be addressed promptly and efficiently.

Moreover, if you desire to gather accurate and up-to-date information about Department of Parks and Recreation Water Safety, simply contact us at *77 on the provided Call Box. Our knowledgeable staff will gladly provide you with valuable resources and guidelines to ensure your safety while enjoying the water.

It is essential to note that, in accordance with the law, individuals who are 21 years old or younger are required to successfully complete an approved Boating Education course. Furthermore, they must carry a Boating Safety Education Card whenever operating a motorboat, including personal watercraft. This safety measure aims to safeguard the well-being of our boaters and ensure responsible practices on the water.

For any further queries or assistance, please do not hesitate to reach out to us. You can send us an email at boatedu@parksandrecreation.idaho.gov. We are committed to providing exceptional boating education and promoting water safety throughout Idaho.

Idaho Tobacco Hotline: 1-800-QUIT NOW (784-8669) is an excellent resource to assist individuals who are looking to quit smoking. Whether you are in need of guidance, support, or simply seeking information about the "IDAT" program, this hotline is here to serve you. Moreover, if you are unable to reach the Idaho Tobacco Hotline, the National Hotline is readily available at 1-800-788-2492 or 1-800-784-8669. These helplines can connect you to programs near your location, ensuring that you receive the assistance you need on your journey towards a tobacco-free life.

Idaho State Police, ISP 1-800-233-1212 or ISP. Alternatively, in the event of an accident, you may contact the Department of Transportation at 1-800-233-1212 for more detailed information. Emergency numbers include *55 for mobile cellular phone users, *477 for those requiring non-emergency roadside assistance, and *ISP for emergencies. CRIME is available to anyone in Idaho who needs comprehensive criminal investigation information. Simply program CRIME into your cellular phone and have unrestricted access to valuable resources (24 hours, 7 days a week). You can also contact the ISP Communication Center at 208-846-7500 for local and other out-of-state cell phone assistance. The center, conveniently located at 700 S. Stratford in Meridian, Idaho, is always ready to provide prompt and efficient assistance.

Agencies

38.1. Important Phone Numbers and Services

Credit Cards - If you happen to misplace or lose your credit card, it is crucial to take immediate action and report it to the major credit card companies. You can reach out for assistance to Visa at (800) 336-8472, MasterCard at (800) MasterCard, and American Express at (800) 528-4800. It is always wise to act swiftly to prevent any unauthorized transactions or potential fraud.

When callers wonder about the meaning behind the phrase "airport noise," their thoughts often gravitate towards the insulation of residential properties or the need for soundproofing in office spaces and recreational areas surrounding an airport. This inclination towards confusion is understandable; however, it is crucial to emphasize that airport noise is an environmental concern that reaches beyond the economic perspective encompassed by the initial question. Airport noise not only impacts the local population by diminishing real estate value, restricting market opportunities, and imposing additional costs in terms of health, maintenance, and education. Its effects go well beyond what is implied solely from an economic standpoint.

Made in United States
Troutdale, OR
12/17/2024

26800833R00093